Doing Their Bit

Ashby de la Zouch Girls' Wartime Harvest Camps 1942-1944

Best wishes
Wendy Freer

Other books by Wendy Freer:

Women and Children of the Cut, 1995,
Railway and Canal Historical Society.

Canal Boatmen's Missions, (with Gill Foster), 2004,
Railway and Canal Historical Society.

Ashby de la Zouch Workhouse and the Ashby Poor Law Union, 2012,
Ashby de la Zouch Museum.

All of a Lather, Soap Manufacture in Ashby de la Zouch 1890-2011
(with Alwyn Owen and Derick Stokes), 2013,
Ashby de la Zouch Museum.

Doing Their Bit

Ashby de la Zouch Girls' Wartime Harvest Camps 1942-1944

Wendy Freer

**Pudding Bag Productions
2015**

Copyright 2015 Wendy Freer

All rights reserved. This book or any portion thereof may not be reproduced or used in any manner whatsoever without the express written permission of the publisher except for the use of brief quotations in a book review or scholarly journal.

First Printing: 2015

ISBN 978-1-326-23994-7

Pudding Bag Productions
68 Wood Street
Ashby de la Zouch
Leicestershire
LE65 1EG

wendyfreer.org.uk

Acknowledgements

I would like to thanks Ashby de la Zouch Museum for permission to reproduce the Ashby Girls' Wartime School Harvest Camp Logbook. The original is held in the Museum archives. Thanks are also due to the Museum of Rural Life at the University of Reading for permission to use the photograph on page 4.

Contents

Introduction	3
1. Harvest Camps and Child labour in World War II	5
2. Ashby Girls' Wartime Harvest Camp, 1942	11
3. Ashby Girls' Wartime Harvest Camp 1943	17
4. Ashby Girls' Wartime Harvest Camp 1944	40
Appendices	
1.1 Roll Call 1942	64
1.2 Hours and Earnings 1942	68
1.3 Camp Cash Account 1942	74
1.4 Orderlies and Field Work 1942	78
2.1 Roll call 1943	80
2.2 Hours and Earnings 1943	85
2.3 Camp Cash Account 1943	91
2.4 Orderlies 1943	95

Ashby de la Zouch Girls' Wartime Harvest Camps 1942-1944

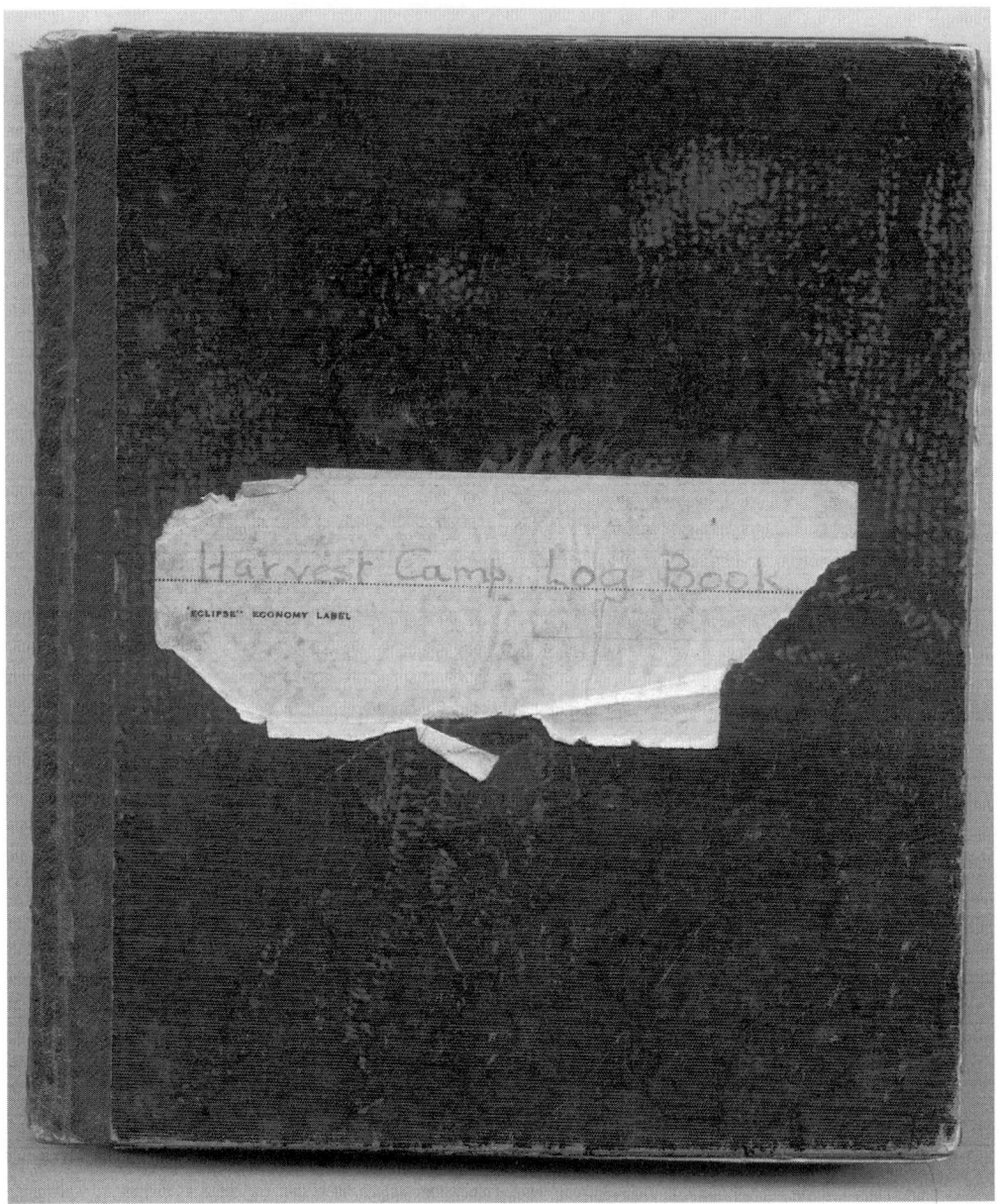

The front cover of the school exercise book used for the Harvest Log

Introduction

During the winter of 2012/2013, Ashby de la Zouch Museum began the task of ordering and cataloguing the Ashby Grammar School material in their archive. By a lucky chance, while materials lay stacked in the Ferrers Community Room awaiting attention, I spotted a battered, hard-covered exercise book, with a fading, peeling label. The title, *Harvest Camp Log Book* was intriguing, the contents even more so. The book was the sole surviving record of the efforts of dozens of teenage girls during the wartime years of 1942, 1943 and 1944, to help bring in the harvest at local farms.

Such harvest camps were set up for boys and girls throughout the country during the Second World War and, without them, it is doubtful whether the nation could have been adequately fed during this period. In the first chapter of this book, you can read more about the background to child labour in agriculture during the war and, in particular, the way in which the harvest camps came about and their contribution to food production. The remaining chapters reproduce in full the diaries kept by the teachers of the Ashby Harvest Camps for girls, which were held at what was then Ashby Girls' Grammar School. In the appendices, I have reproduced the roll call records and accounts of hours worked and earnings. Family historians may find the names included therein useful.

In 1942, the teacher responsible for keeping the log made only the briefest account of the day-to-day events. In 1943, a fuller account of day-to-day activities was kept, but the real gem is the 1944 diary. It not only describes, in fascinating detail, the work and the social activities in the camp, but is also delightfully illustrated with pencil drawings showing the farming activities, the tennis and cricket matches and even the Italian prisoners of war! It is amazing that this record, made long ago by anonymous teachers, has survived; the insight it gives us into this aspect of Ashby history is invaluable.

During the Second World War, everyone, even children, was expected to "do their bit" for the war effort. "Bit" hardly seems an appropriate word for the backbreaking work which these girls undertook, working up to 30 hours a week during their summer holidays. I am so pleased that, through the publication of this book, their efforts will not now be forgotten.

Ashby de la Zouch Girls' Wartime Harvest Camps 1942-1944

This photograph is not of the Ashby camp but shows schoolgirls, girl guides and members of the Girls Training Corps picking field beans during a wartime harvest camp.

(photo courtesy of Museum of English Rural Life, University of Reading, PFW PH2/W13/24)

Wendy Freer

1. Harvest Camps and Child Labour in World War II

During the Second World War, the need to feed the population of the United Kingdom led to thousands of acres of pasture being turned over to arable cultivation. Between 1941 and 1944, the acreage of permanent grassland declined by 34% from 1938 levels. The area cropped by potatoes alone increased by 92% on pre-war levels and many thousands of acres were given over to the growing of wheat, other grain and root crops. At the same time, labour to work on the land and bring in the harvest was hemorrhaging at an alarming rate as men joined the armed forces or went to work in construction or munitions to support the war effort. Irish labour, which had formerly been used on farms, was also unavailable during the war. Agriculture was not a protected occupation at the start of the war, although, in June 1940, the Ministry of Labour was empowered to prohibit employers in other occupations from engaging male agricultural workers. The Women's Land Army was only a small force in the early years of the conflict, and prisoners of war were in short supply until after a successful campaign in North Africa, led by General Sir Archibald Wavell in the winter of 1940-41.

Adult Harvest Camps

The problem of how to bring in the harvest of 1940 was addressed largely by the use of volunteer labour. Voluntary Land Clubs were set up for people to help on farms at weekends and, by 1943, over a thousand harvest camps had been established for adults. Volunteers were housed in buildings of various kinds; one volunteer recalls being accommodated in Alne Hall in Yorkshire[1].

They were paid at rates set by County Agricultural Wages Boards from which they had to pay for their keep but, according to the Alne Hall volunteer, people didn't expect to make money. They went out of patriotism and a strong desire to "do their bit" for the war effort. Staying for a week or two, they usually slept in bunk beds in makeshift dormitories, were fed on plain but hearty food, and sometimes treated to ENSA concerts. With much of the coast out of bounds, and the beaches full of barbed wire and mines, the Ministry of Agriculture hoped that people would choose to go on a harvest camp instead of their usual summer holiday and it wasn't disappointed; the response was massive. Recruiting centres were set up in shops, factories and offices and people could also apply to the Ministry of Agriculture. They would be sent a list of camps from which to choose. Employers were also urged to stagger workers' holidays so that some would be available outside the usual holiday months of July and August to help with the potato harvest in the autumn. Wet conditions in the summer of 1944 made the potato harvest particularly problematic with the number of volunteers dropping off at the prospect of back-breaking work in the rain and mud and few, if any, military personnel available. In Leicestershire, Nottinghamshire and Lincolnshire, school children were given extra leave to help and, in other parts of the country, more prisoners of war were drafted in.

The use of children for farm work

In rural districts, it had long been the practice for children to help with various tasks on farms and, at critical times of the year, such as the main potato harvest in the autumn, the education authorities often turned a blind eye to school absence. During the Second World War, this unofficial use of child labour was greatly increased. Just as adult civilians were being asked to "Dig for Victory' by growing food in their gardens, schools were encouraged to turn over any pieces of land they had for the same thing. Some kept livestock such as pigs and some even "adopted" local farms. Before long, urban children were becoming involved, at first when they were evacuated to the countryside, but soon in other ways, including the setting up of holiday-time harvest camps.

In 1941, Local Education Authorities were instructed to adjust school holidays to coincide with critical points in the farming year. In Leicestershire, the normal summer holiday was shortened to allow children to be released for three weeks in October to help with the potato harvest[2].

Proposals to use child labour in agriculture during term time, even on a purely voluntary basis, met with objections from both teaching and farming unions. Some thought that there was a danger of farmers exploiting children as a source of cheap, un-unionised labour. Some teaching staff thought that it would lead to a breakdown of school discipline. Despite objections, the use of child labour during term time was legalised by an Order in Council on 5th May 1942. Under this Order, children were permitted to work for a maximum of 20 half days per year, provided there was no compulsion, permission was granted by a father, close relative or evacuation billeting householder and children did not work more than four hours in any one day. Children were to receive the minimum agricultural wage and no child under fourteen was to be employed until all sources of adult labour had been exhausted.

The scheme was very successful and children made a particularly significant contribution to the potato harvest between 1941 and 1944. After that, the use of prisoners of war took some of the pressure off but, by 1947, it was necessary to reinstate the scheme, which ran until it was discontinued in 1950.

Harvest Camps for Children

Harvest camps for boys started to be set up by both state secondary and public schools in 1940. However, because of their *ad hoc and* unofficial nature, there was a problem with financing them. At between 6d (2½p) and 8d (3.3p) per hour, the boys' earnings were barely enough to cover their travel costs and contributions to their keep. There was usually no insurance cover and, often, inadequate supervision.

In 1940, the Ministry of Agriculture consulted head teachers' associations and, the following year, set up a series of Departmental Committees to address the issues and consider putting them on a more formal footing. This was followed, in 1942, by the setting up of the Schoolboy Harvest Camps Advisory Committee (SHCAC) under the Chairmanship of Robert Hyde, Director of the Industrial Welfare Society[3]. In the same year, government help was given with the cost of rail fares to the camps, and accommodation was provided free of charge[4].

At most camps, children were accommodated under canvas but, in some, they slept in schools, church halls or nissan huts and, occasionally, country houses and castles. In all cases, huge amounts of equipment had to be borrowed or hired, such as palliasses (stuffed with straw), blankets and camp beds. In camps housed in tents, cooking equipment, buckets, food bins, storm lamps, kettles, boilers, trestle tables and latrine screens also had to be found. Schools with a camping tradition could use their own equipment and the Ministry of Agriculture would pay them an agreed sum for depreciation. As well as organising equipment, transport and finance, suitable locations had to be found with attention given to the safety of the children. There was concern over the danger from aerial bombardment and, in Sussex, one boy was fired on by German fighters while picking swedes[5]! At the end of each camp, everything had to be dismantled, cleaned and, in some cases, transported to another part of the country for use in other seasonal harvests; early potatoes and peas in early summer, grain harvest in high summer and main crop potato picking in the autumn. The optimum size for camps was generally thought to be 25 to 30 children, 2 teachers and 2 cooks but the Ashby camps grew to be much bigger. The cooks would sometimes be volunteers such as teachers' wives. In some camps, there was additional adult help such as orderlies but in others (including Ashby) the orderlies were the children themselves. The whole operation took a great deal of organisation and the advice given by the SHCAC was vital.

Camps were supposed to be self-financing with the children's earnings covering all costs. With luck, there would be a surplus which would be divided between the participants so that children could go home with some money in their pockets. However, if the weather was bad, and farm work was not available, this could result in substantial losses. In 1942, the Ministry of Agriculture persuaded the Treasury to allow a block grant to be used to make up boys' pay to a guaranteed 30 hour's work even where inclement weather had made work impossible. Schools were also allowed to hire camping equipment free of charge from the Office of Works. At its peak, in 1944, total Treasury expenditure on boys' harvest camps was £56,000 (£2.25 million approx. 2015 equivalent).

At first, it was not felt worthwhile to hold harvest camps for girls as they were not thought physically capable of such heavy work. Furthermore, it was expected that girls' camps would cost more as females were thought to need more latrines and sickbay space. Doubts about the ability of girls to make a significant contribution to the harvest soon proved to be unfounded. Most farmers very much appreciated the help given by children, and especially by girls who were felt to be more enthusiastic and keener to learn. Camps for girls got underway in 1942 and, in 1943, over 20,000 girls took part, but there were always far more camps for boys.

As well as the contribution to the war effort and the feeding of the nation, the value of the camps was seen to be cultural, social and educational as urban children got their first experience of country life and children from different social backgrounds were brought into contact with each other. Even when financial help with travel costs was available, however, it wasn't always easy for urban children from poor backgrounds to take part. Lack of suitable footwear was a particular problem and, in Leicestershire, Lord Cromwell approached the government to ask if child harvesters could be provided with extra clothing coupons. This request was turned down.

Feeding children who were ravenously hungry after a day of hard work in the open air could also be a problem and, sometimes, not only food, but volunteer cooks, were in short supply. In 1943, an appeal was made to students at Domestic Science Colleges to help in return for free board and lodging and payment of 30 shillings a week. The response was good and the Ministry of Food and the Board of Education both issued books of advice on catering for harvest camps. The minimum wage, regardless of the task, was supposed to be 8d per hour for 16 year olds and 6d per hour for younger children. However, camp organisers were within their rights to ask for more where conditions dictated and farmers were duty bound to pay. In 1946, the hourly minimum rate for children aged 14 to 19 was raised to 9d.

The basic weekly diet in the camps for children was supposed to be 8oz (227g) cheese, 2lbs (907g) tinned meat, 1lb (454g) canned beans, ½lb (227g) of biscuits, 2oz (57g) dried fruit, rice "as required" and unspecified amounts of New Zealand honey. This was supplemented with local supplies of fruit and vegetables, rabbits and milk. In 1944, the meat rations were reduced and rations of cheese and egg powder increased to compensate.

The daily routine in the camp was strictly regimented, as will be seen from the "Rules" (see page 12-13) and the "General Order of the Day"(see pages 19-21) posted up at Ashby Grammar School and recorded in the log. Rising at 7am, there would be prayers and breakfast and then walk or cycle to the farm where work was to take place. Work was usually over by 5pm and there would be some time for socialising and recreation as well as a hot evening meal and lights out between 9 and 10pm.

R. J. Moore-Colyer, who wrote the article *Kids in the Corn: School Harvest Camps and farm labour supply in England, 1940–1950* for the Agricultural History Review in 2004, has been the main source of information for this chapter. He subsequently took part in a BBC Radio 4 programme on the subject, (*Making History*) and was inundated afterwards with emails and letters containing memories and even essays poems and drawings of the camps from all over the United Kingdom. This led him to write a short follow-up article in 2006 in which he summarised some of them[5]. As well as describing the work, and attitudes to it, he reproduces some of the recollections of the social side of the camps. Italian prisoners of war, he writes, could make life interesting. Although some boys resented having to work alongside prisoners, girls found the Italians' dark hair, eyes and complexions exciting and attractive! Two girls at a Lutterworth camp spent a lot of time chatting to them in Latin! Italian prisoners of war are mentioned in our Ashby log and one can imagine that the reaction of our sixth formers to them was probably very similar! Although some of the participants who contacted Moore-Colyer hated their time in camp, the overwhelming impression was one of enjoyment and pride in having "done their bit" for the war effort and this is also what comes across from the Ashby Harvest Log.

Girls came to Ashby from Birmingham, Stafford and other parts of Leicestershire. They certainly worked hard, but recreation and socializing – even with the boys at Ashby Grammar School Harvest Camp – were a regular feature. Although there is at least one mention of homesickness, most girls seem to have enjoyed themselves. Why else would girls who were pupils at Ashby Grammar School, and who could have worked from home, have joined the camps as residents?

notes

1. BBC The People's War
   http://www.bbc.co.uk/history/ww2peopleswar/stories/95/a2222795.shtml
2. Moore-Colyer, R. J. *Kids in the Corn: school harvest camps and farm labour supply in England, 1940-1950,* Agricultural History Review, vol 52, part II, 2004, p.191.
3. Parliamentary Debates, Commons, 377, 1941-2 Jan 192
4. Gosden, Peter, *Education in the Second World War: A Study in Policy and Administration,* 1976, pp.80-82
5. Moore-Colyer, R. J. *Children's Labour in the Countryside during World War II: a further note,* Agricultural History Review, Vol. 54, II, 2006, p.333.

Wendy Freer

2 Ashby Girls' Wartime Harvest Camp 1942

In 1942, the girls' harvest camp appears to have run for four weeks from 16th August to 12th September. Girls slept in the Ashby Girls' Grammar School Building in rooms 1, 1A and the library. A log was kept for the first ten days only and it makes the very briefest record of which farms were involved and an indication of the work undertaken. The actual log, and a transcript, can be seen on the following pages together with the camp rules as set down in the logbook. In the final week of the camp a very brief note of work undertaken was also kept and this can be seen in Appendix 1.4.

During the first week of the camp, 20 girls were present (see Roll Call in Appendix 1.1) with two staff members. There is no record of where they came from. Numbers swelled slightly to 22 in the second and third week but dropped to 15 (including one non-resident) in the fourth week. It is rather surprising that girls were still resident as late as the second week in September when one would have thought the school term had restarted.

A total of 33 individual girls took part in the camps over the four weeks. Most (19) stayed for two weeks, nine stayed for three weeks and three hardy souls stayed for the full four weeks. Two girls left after only a week.

The earnings sheets can be seen in Appendices 1.2 to this book. The figure after their names on the earnings sheet is their age, showing that there were nine 14 year olds, eight 15 year olds, two 16 year olds and one 17 year old. It would appear that work began on Monday of that week with some girls working a half day of three hours and some a full day of six hours. The figures also suggest that on Monday and Tuesday, staff applied different wage rates for girls aged 16 and over (7d per hour) and those under 16 (5½ d per hour) although for the remainder of the week, all girls appear to have been paid at the same rate. The differentiated rates of pay are, however, confirmed on another page entitled *Received from Employers* (Appendix 1.2) which shows that the girls were working on flax pulling and potato pulling.

Another page (Appendix 1.3) shows the amount of money each girl was paid, or perhaps drew out, at the end of the week. Some drew out significantly more than others but the facing page (Receipts) suggests that some girls brought pocket money with them which is presumably why they were able to draw out more than others.

Ashby de la Zouch Girls' Wartime Harvest Camps 1942-1944

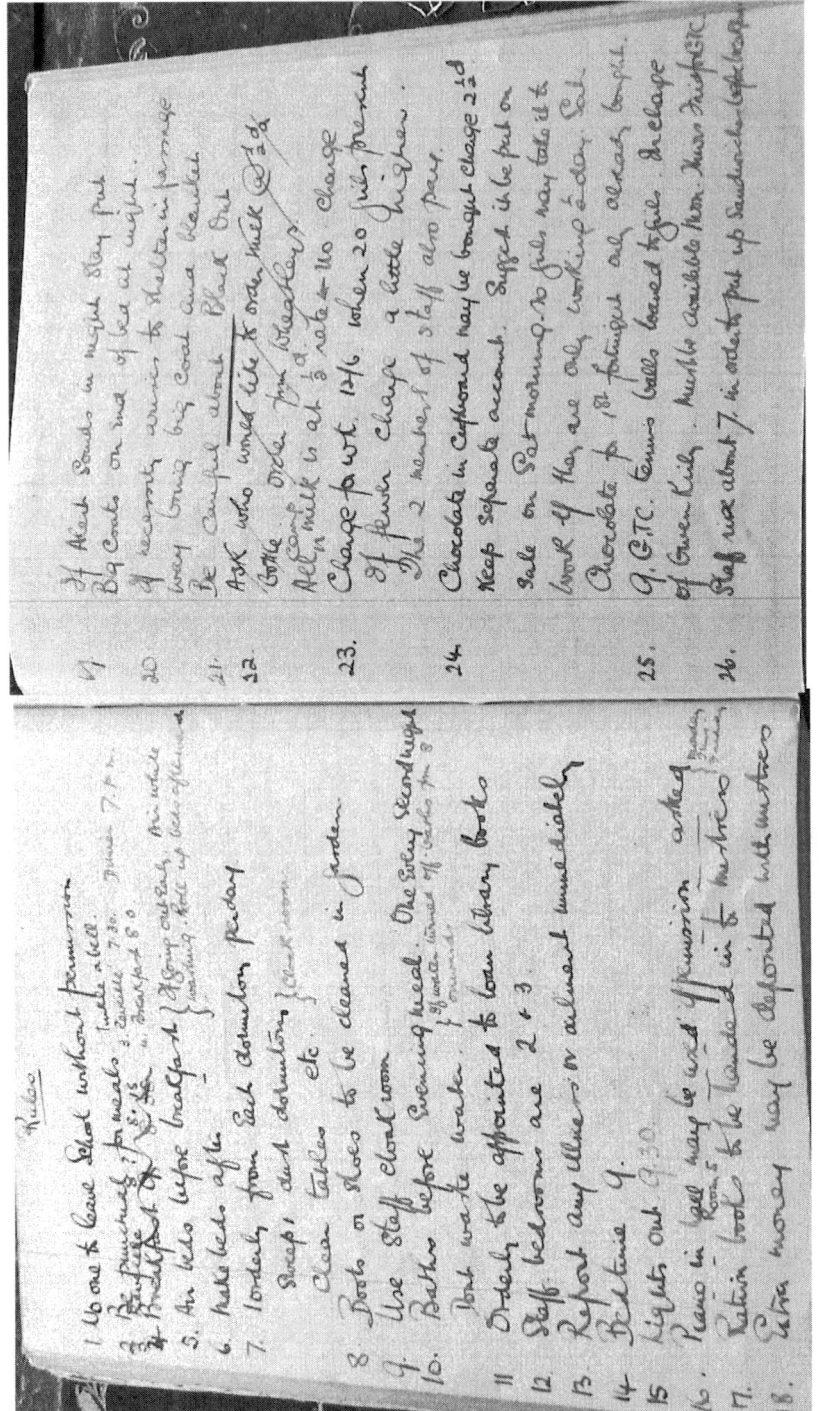

Above: Camp rules for 1942. Transcript on opposite page.

Wendy Freer

Rules

1. No-one to leave school without permission
2. Be punctual for meals
3. Reveille 7.30
4. Breakfast 8am   dinner 7pm
5. Air beds before breakfast. If going out early, air while washing. Roll up beds afterwards.
6. Make beds after breakfast.
7. 1 orderly from each dormitory per day sweep, dust dormitory, clean tables etc. cloakroom.
8. Boots or shoes to be cleaned in garden.   9. Use staff cloakroom.
10. Baths before evening meal. One every second night. Don't waste water. If water turned off, baths from 8 onwards.
11. Orderly to be appointed to loan library books.
12. Staff bedrooms are 2 and 3.
13. Report any illness or ailment immediately.
14. Bedtime 9.   15. Lights out 9.30.
16. Piano in hall and room 5 may be used if permission asked.
17. Ration books to be handed in to mistresses.
18. Extra money may be deposited with mistresses.
19. If Alert sounds in night stay put. Big coats on end of bed at night.
20. If necessity arises to shelter in passage, bring big coat and blanket.
21. Be careful about black out.
22. All camp milk is at ½d rate – no charge.
23. Charge for week 12/6 when 20 girls present. If fewer, charge a little higher. The two members of staff also pay.
24. Chocolate in cupboard may be bought. Charge 2½d. Keep separate account. Suggest it be put on sale on Sat morning so girls may take it to work if they are only working ½ day. Sat chocolate for first fortnight only already bought.
25. A.C.T.C. (Ashby Castle Tennis Club) tennis balls loaned to girls. In charge of Gwen Kirby. Must be available Mon Thurs Fri for CTC (tennis club.)
26. Staff rise at about 7 in order to put up sandwiches before breakfast.

Ashby de la Zouch Girls' Wartime Harvest Camps 1942-1944

> Farm Orders for.
> Monday 17th August   7. at cheap rate for
> Breach Farm (Robeys) at 9.
> Miss Champion 3. at 2. To clean garage.
> Tuesday 18th August. 7 at cheap rate for Breach Farm.
> 18th August   12 for Breach Farm 1-30 p.m. approx
> Wednesday 19th August 20 for Breach Farm
> Thursday 20th   "   20
> Friday 21st   "   20
> Saturday   19
>
> Monday 24th. All available for Ottewell Farm. Mr
> ~~Keith's~~ for flax pulling. 9.30. (About
> 1 mile up Nottingham Rd on L.H.S. pile one before you
> reach the house). One member of staff to be there all the time.
> On Monday there is an official supervisor, but each of Ashby Staff
> should drop in to see what will be expected on future days
> Tuesday. 25th 16 for Ottewell Farm.
>   5 under 16 for Mr. Hewitt,
>   potato lifting.

Above: Camp log 1942. Transcript opposite.

Wendy Freer

Camp log

Monday 17th August 1942

7 at cheap rate for Breach Farm[1] (Robey's) at 9

Miss Champion, 3 at 2 to clean garage.

Tuesday 18th August 1942

7 at cheap rate for Breach Farm

12 for Breach Farm 1.30 pm approx.

Wednesday 19th August 1942

20 for Breach Farm

Thursday 20th August 1942

20 for Breach Farm

Friday 21st August 1942

20 for Breach Farm

Saturday 22nd August 1942

19 for Breach Farm

Monday 24th August 1942

All available for Ottewell Farm[2] for flax pulling 9.30 (about 1 mile up Nottingham Road on left-hand side field one before you reach the house). One member of staff to be there all the time. On Monday there is an official supervisor, but each of Ashby staff should drop in to see what will be expected on future days.

Tuesday 25th August 1942

16 for Ottewell Farm

5 under 16 for Mr Hewitt, potato lifting.

---

[1] Breach Farm lies off the Leicester Road between Corkscrew Lane and Alton Grange
[2] Ottewells Farm is off the Nottingham Road and is now better known as Eastern Old Parks Farm.

Ashby de la Zouch Girls' Wartime Harvest Camps 1942-1944

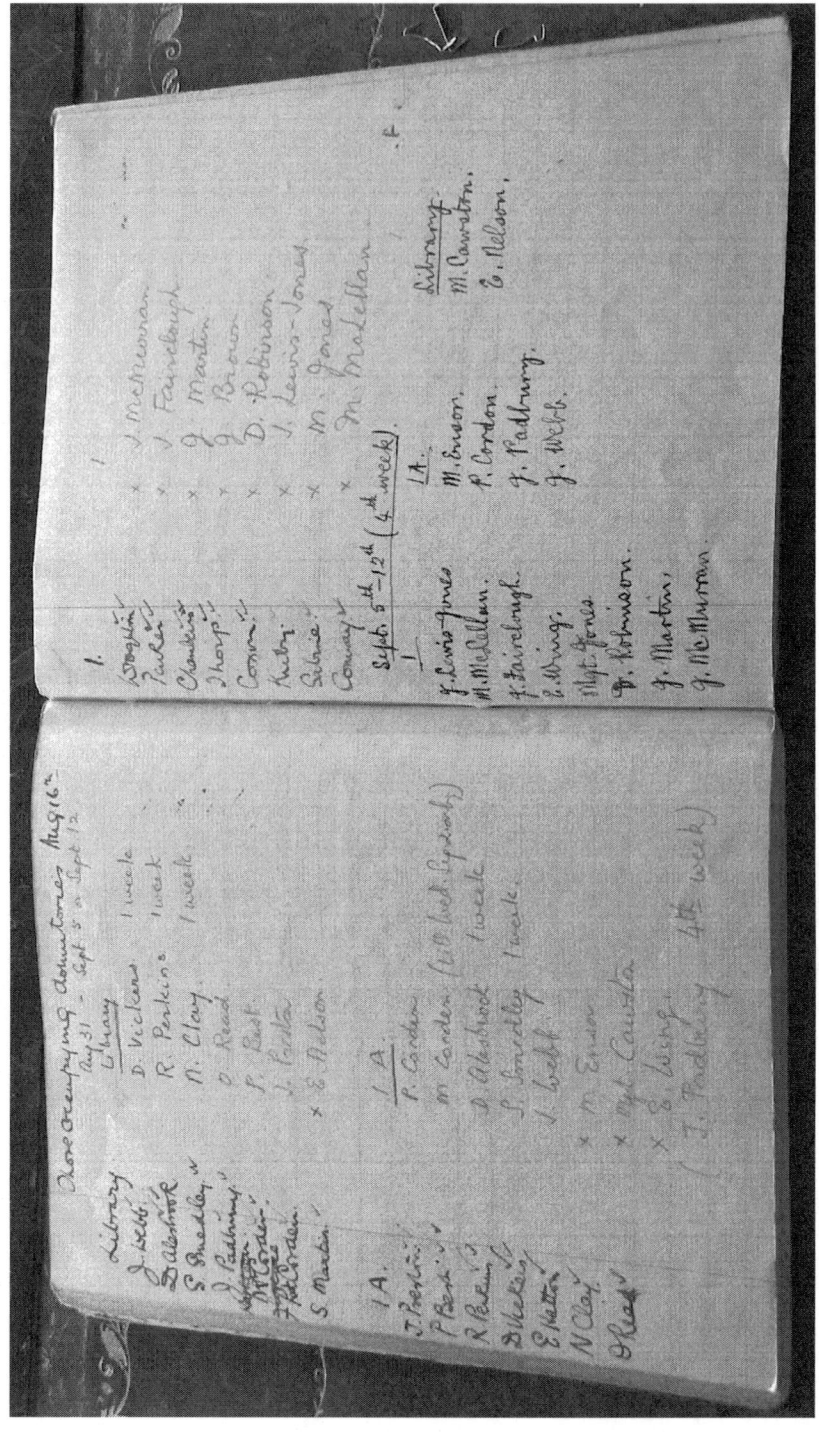

Above: Dormitory allocation, 1942

Wendy Freer

3 Ashby Girls' Wartime Harvest Camp 1943

In 1943, the Harvest Camps began on Monday, August 9th and ended on Saturday, September 4th. It got off to a fairly slow start, with only 20 girls in attendance, four of them working from home. The numbers more than doubled in the second week with 44 girls in camp; there were 48 in the third week and 36 in the final week.

Attendance
Of the 20 girls who came in the first week, 8 stayed on for a further two weeks and one hardy soul stayed for the full four weeks. 10 of the girls who came in the first week went away at the end of the week but came back for another week or more later on.

In the third week, there were only four new girls, most having arrived in the preceding weeks and so were "old hands". In fact, one can recognize quite a number of names in the roll calls as being of those who had attended the previous year and had returned to help again. The final week was evenly divided between newcomers and those who had been there in the previous weeks.

During the whole period of the camps in 1943, several girls went home early. One was called away because of visitors arriving at home, others were sent home suffering from various ailments such as earache, sunstroke and, not surprisingly, sheer exhaustion! Some naughty girls were sent home for smoking in the dorm!

Hours and earnings
The records show that a full day's work was usually reckoned to be six hours, but this was not worked every day. Weather conditions and the availability of work led to a fair amount of variation in hours.

In the first week, the girls worked 5½ hours on Monday and Tuesday, only 2 hours on Wednesday and six hours on Thursday and Friday. It appears that Saturday was always a half day, if it was worked at all, and these hours were carried forward to the following week and accounted for separately.

The second week was the busiest with a full 6 hours being worked every day from Monday to Friday, but on the third week, a 4½ hour day on Friday reduced the overall weekday hours to 28½.

Even fewer hours were worked in the final week with no work being done on Thursday and a number of girls leaving early.

The method of recording and accounting for hours worked is rather difficult to understand. For some reason, in the third week, Friday's hours were counted separately, and what would appear to be a half day on Saturday 21st August carried forward. To make matters worse, although the teachers recorded the day of the week correctly, they sometimes got the date wrong as, for example, in the first week when Monday 9th August was recorded as 8th August in both the log and the accounts and, consequently, all the following dates of that week are also incorrect.

In the accounts for week three, it states at the top of the page that the girls were being paid 8d per hour (3.3p in modern decimal currency). However, the figures for wages show that they were not all paid at the same rate. This is probably because some were aged 16 or over but no ages are given in the records. An amount for board and lodging was deducted, which according to a note in week two, was 11 shillings and 6 pence (55.5p). This was a slight reduction on the 1942 rate, reflecting the larger numbers.

Field work and day-to-day notes
These are a little more detailed than in 1942. Photographs and transcripts can be seen on the pages which follow.

Wendy Freer

General Order of the Day.

- 7.0 a.m. Reveillé – beds open for airing.
- 7.45 – to 8.20. Morning prayer (in Dining Hall). Breakfast
- 8.30 – 9. Make beds, Tidy rooms.
- 9.0. Report for work.

- 5.0 or 6.0. Quick wash and tea.
  Tea time to supper time. – free time and baths.
- 7.0. Supper.
- 7.45 – 9 Free time.
- 9.0. Prepare for bed.
- 9.30. Lights out. (with short evening prayer in big hall).

General Arrangements

Meals. In Dining Hall.

Common Room Biology Lab for reading, letter writing, wireless etc.

Sleeping: In the two K.G. rooms, and large Hall.

Cloak rooms:

1. Girls in K.G. rooms use the Junior Sch. Cloak Rooms. Hang outdoor clothes on stand by windows; towels and sponge bags on stand near clock. Choose a peg and keep it for the week. (no towels etc in bedrooms) Use the inner part for washing and lavatory — if after dark, see that ventilator is shut because of black out.

2. Girls in the large hall use the big cloak room for outdoor clothes and staff cloak room (or later small cloak room) for towels and sponge bags. Choose a peg and keep it for the week.

   Both staff and girls' washing bowls and lavatories of the downstairs cloak rooms may be used.

Baths Unfortunately water is turned off <u>all evening</u>; but we hope to collect enough hot water for all girls in turn to have a hot bath in the zinc baths. Each girl should empty her own bath, wipe it out and leave ready for the next girl.

Wendy Freer

General Order of the Day

7 am	Reveille – beds open for airing
7.45 to 8.30	Morning prayer (in Dining Hall) Breakfast
8.30 – 9am	Make beds. Tidy rooms.
9am	Report for work
5 or 6pm	Quick wash and tea
	Teatime to suppertime, free time and baths.
7pm	Supper
7.45 – 9pm	Free time
9pm	Prepare for bed
9.30	Lights out (with short evening prayer in big Hall)

General Arrangements

Meals in Dining Hall

Common Room Biology lab for reading, letter writing, wireless etc.

Sleeping In the two K.G. rooms and large Hall

Cloakrooms Girls in K.G. rooms use the junior school cloakrooms. Hang outdoor clothes on stand by windows; towels and sponge bags near clock. Choose a peg and keep it for the week. (no towels in bedrooms). Use the inner part [of the washroom] for washing and lavatory. If after dark, see that ventilator is shut because of blackout.
Girls in the large hall use the big cloakroom for outdoor clothes and staff cloakroom (or later small cloakroom) for towels and sponge bags. Choose a peg and keep it for the week. Both staff and girls' washing bowls and lavatories of the downstairs cloakrooms may be used.

Baths Unfortunately water is turned off all evening but we hope to collect enough hot water for all girls in turn to have a hot bath in the zinc baths. Each girl should empty her own bath, wipe it out and leave ready for the next girl.

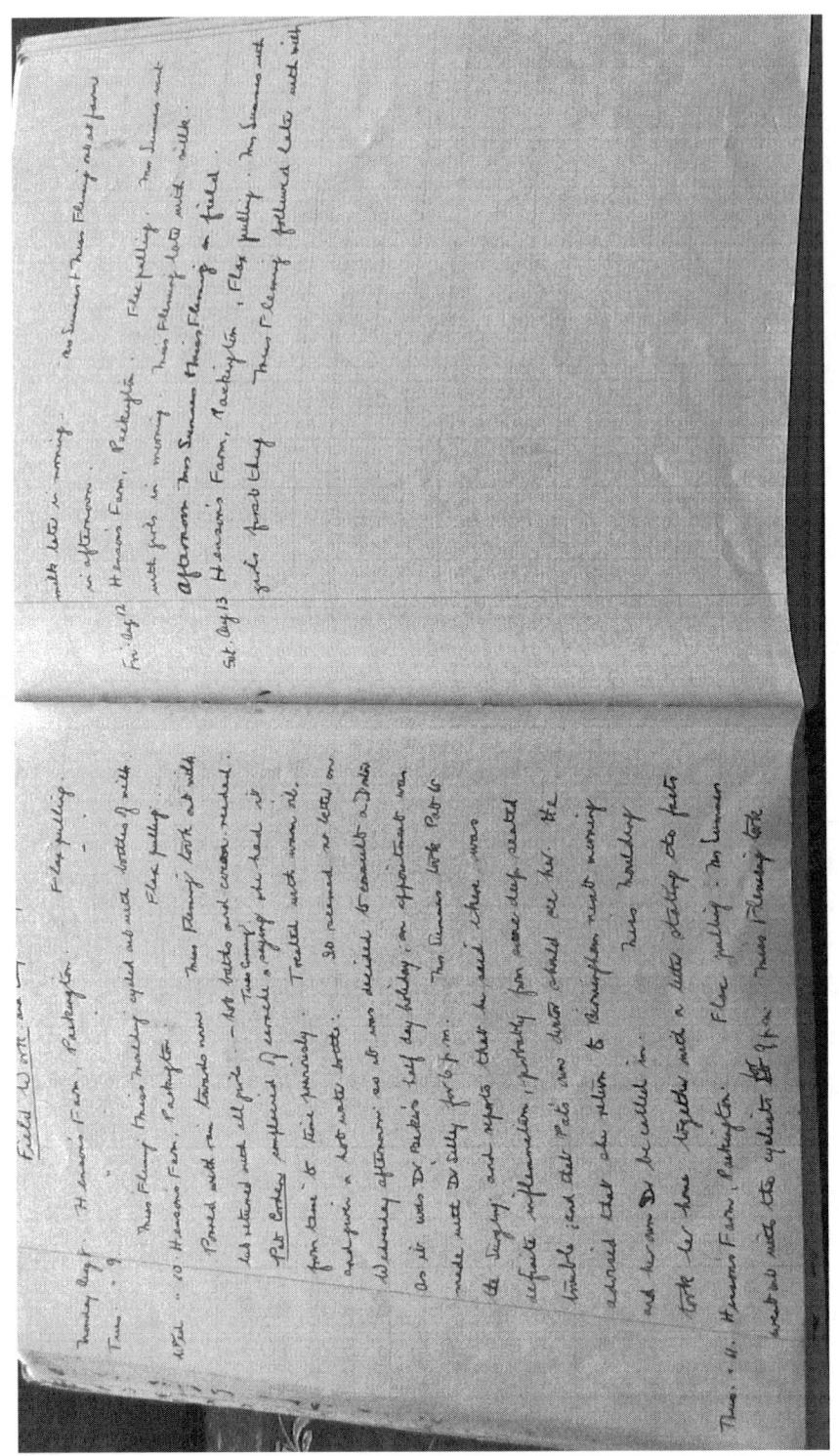

Wendy Freer

Field Work and day-to-day notes 1943

Monday August 8th (*sic, this date should read Monday August 9th. The staff seem to have got muddled up with the dates.*)

Henson's Farm, Packington, flax pulling.

Tuesday August 9th
Miss Fleming and Miss Moulding cycled out with bottles of milk.

Wednesday August 10th
Henson's farm, Packington, flax pulling. Poured with rain towards noon. Miss Fleming took out milk but returned with all girls – hot baths and cocoa needed. Pat Corden complained of earache Tuesday evening, saying she had it from time to time previously. Treated with warm oil and given a hot water bottle. It seemed no better on Wednesday afternoon so it was decided to consult a Doctor. As it was Dr. Baker's half day holiday, an appointment was made with Dr. Silly for 6pm. Miss (or Mrs?) Summers took Pat to the surgery and reported that he said there was a definite inflammation, probably from some deep-seated trouble and that Pat's own doctor should see her. He advised that she return to Birmingham next morning and her own doctor be called in. Miss Moulding took her home, together with a letter stating the facts.

Thursday August 11th
Henson's farm, Packington. Flax pulling. Miss Summers went out with the cyclists for 9am. Miss Fleming took milk later in morning. Miss Summers, Miss Fleming at farm in afternoon.

Friday August 12th
Henson's farm Packington. Flax pulling. Miss Summers out with girls in morning. Miss Fleming later with milk. Afternoon, Miss Summers, Miss Fleming in field.

Saturday August 13th
Henson's Farm Packington, flax pulling. Mrs Summers with girls first thing. Miss Fleming followed later with milk.

[From the following week, another teacher takes over the log and she obviously does know the correct date!]

Ashby de la Zouch Girls' Wartime Harvest Camps 1942-1944

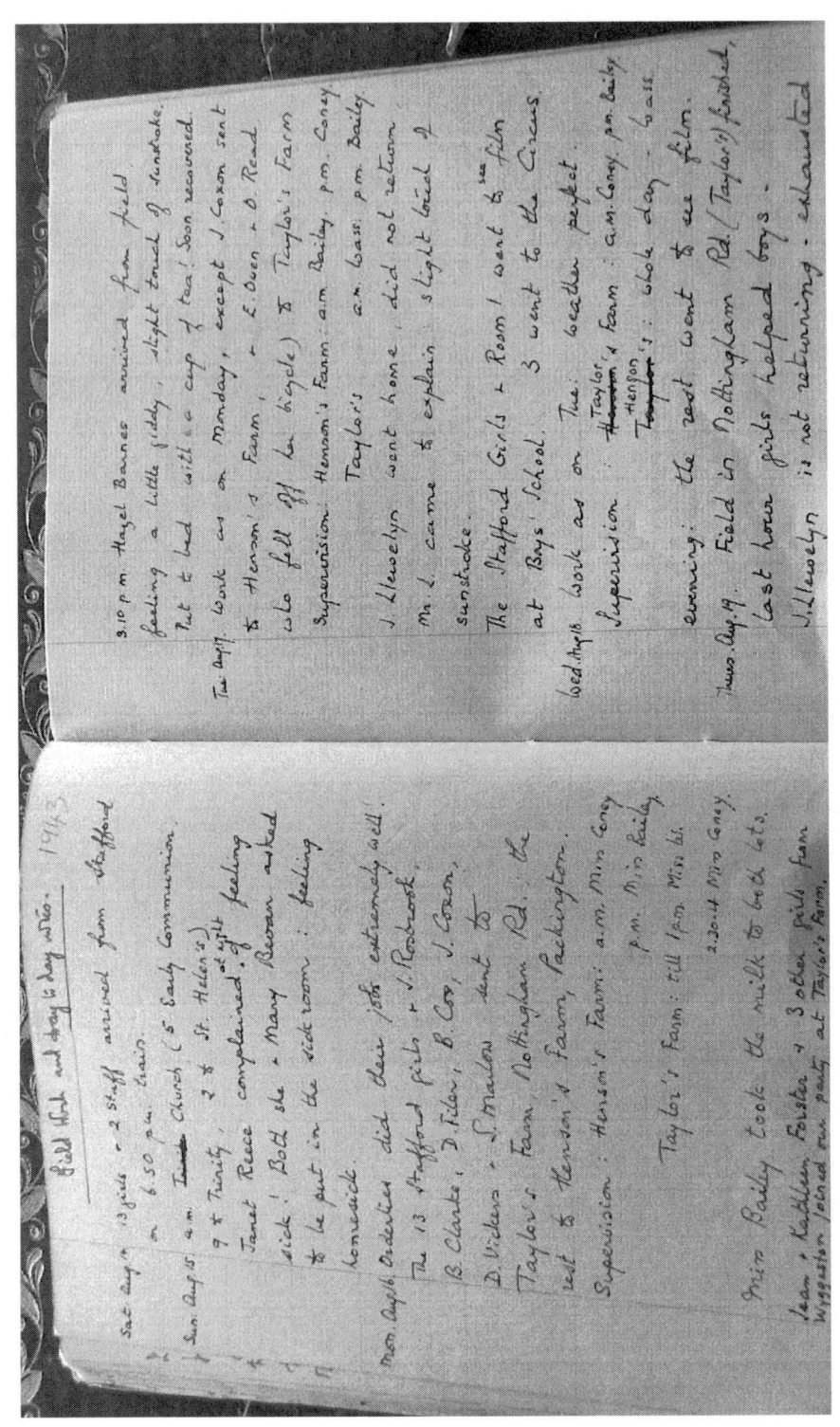

Field Work and day to day note - 1943

Sat Aug 7 13 girls + 2 staff arrived from Stafford on 6.50 p.m. train.

Sun Aug 10 a.m. Trinity Church (5 Early Communion, 7 t Trinity. 2 t St Helen's) Janet Reece complained of feeling sick. Both she + Mary Rowan asked to be put in the sick room; feeling homesick.

Mon Aug 11 6 Veterans did their jobs extremely well. The 13 Stafford girls + J. Pinchbeck B. Clarke, D. Filer, B. Cox, J. Coxon, D. Videns + S. Marlow sent to Taylor's Farm, Nottingham Rd, the rest to Henson's Farm, Packington. Supervision: Henson's Farm: a.m. Miss Coney p.m. Miss Bailey Taylor's Farm: till 1 p.m. Miss Wt. 2.30 at Miss Gray.

Miss Bailey took the milk to bed lots.

Jean + Kathleen Forster + 3 other girls from Wigginton joined our party at Taylor's Farm.

3.10 p.m. Hazel Barnes arrived from field feeling a little giddy, slight touch of sunstroke. Put to bed with a cup of tea. Soon recovered.

Tue Aug 12 All work as on Monday, except J. Coxon sent to Henson's Farm, + E. Owen + D. Read (who fell off her bicycle) to Taylor's Farm Supervision. Henson's Farm: a.m. Bailey p.m. Coney Taylor's a.m. Bass p.m. Bailey

J. Llewelyn went home. did not return. M.L. came to explain. slight touch of sunstroke.

The Stafford Girls + Room 1 went to see film at Boys' School. 3 went to the Circus.

Wed Aug 13 Work as on Tue. Weather perfect.
Supervision: Taylor's Farm: a.m. Coney p.m. Bailey Henson's: whole day - Bass

evening: the rest went to see film.

Thurs Aug 14 Field in Nottingham Rd. (Taylor's) finished. Last hour girls helped boys -
J. Llewelyn is not returning - exhausted

Field Work and day-to-day notes

Saturday August 14th
13 girls and 2 staff arrived from Stafford on 6.50 p.m. train.

Sunday August 15th
Church (5 Early Communion, 9 to Trinity, 2 to St Helen's) Janet Reece complained at night of feeling sick! Both she and Mary Bevan asked to be put in the sick room: feeling homesick.

Monday August 16th
Orderlies did their jobs extremely well. The 13 Stafford girls & J Rosbrook, B Clarke, D Filer, B Cox, J Coxon, D Vickers, S Marlow sent to Taylor's Farm, Nottingham Rd. The rest to Henson's Farm, Packington.

Supervision: Henson's Farm,   a.m. Miss Coney
                                         p.m. Bailey
                 Taylor's Farm, till 1 p.m. Miss W.
                                     2.30 to 4 Miss Coney

Miss Bailey took the milk to both lots. Jean and Kathleen Foster and 3 other girls from Wyggeston joined our party at Taylor's Farm.

3.10 p.m. Hazel Barnes arrived from field feeling a little giddy, slight touch of sunstroke. Put to bed with a cup of tea! Soon recovered.

Tuesday August 17th
Work as on Monday, except J Coxon sent to Henson's Farm and E Owen and O Read (who fell off her bicycle) to Taylor's Farm.

Supervision: Henson's Farm, a.m. Bailey, p.m. Coney
                 Taylor's,   a.m. Wass, p.m. Bailey

J Llewelyn went home, did not return. Mr L came to explain slight touch of sunstroke.

The Stafford girls in Room 1 went to see a film at Boys' School. 3 went to the Circus.

Wednesday August 18th
Work as on Tuesday. Weather perfect.
Supervision: Taylor's Farm, a.m. Coney, p.m. Bailey
Henson's, whole day, Wass   Evening: the rest went to see film.

Thursday August 19th
Field in Nottingham Road (Taylor's) finished. Last hour, girls helped boys. J Llewelyn is not returning, exhausted [continued on next page]

Field Work & Day to day notes (cont)

after the few days' flax pulling.
Tennis & dancing in Room 16 —
mixed.
Supervision: a.m. Henson & p.m. Bailey p.m. Wass
Taylor's & Corey p.m. Bailey

Fri: Aug.20. All worked in Packington.
1943 Supervision: a.m. Wass. p.m. Corey.
Only 1½ hours' work in the afternoon.
S. Marlow on way back must have
fainted, fell off bicycle dragging
P. Best with her — was picked up by car,
brought home. Washed, put to bed,
(zambuk applied for cuts) & given
hot tea & later aspirins. Both soon
recovered. Sheila remained in sick room.
Girls invited to social at A.B.G.S.

Aug.21. All worked for 1 hr. only, owing to rain,
at Packington.
P. Best, S. Marlow & A. Sabine stayed behind.
E. Jaws, M. Jackson, E. Nelson, J. Preston, M. Jones,
D. Elvey employed by farmer for stooking.

[continued from previous page] after the few days' flax pulling.

Tennis and dancing in Room 16 – mixed.

Supervision:	a.m. Henson's, Bailey, p.m. Wass
Taylor's Coney, p.m. Bailey

Friday August 20th

All worked in Packington.

Supervision: a.m. Wass   p.m. Coney

Only 1½ hours' work in the afternoon. S Marlow on way back must have fainted, fell off bicycle dragging P Best with her – was picked up by car, brought home, washed, put to bed (Zambuk applied for cuts) and given hot tea and later asprins. Both soon recovered. Sheila remained in sickroom. Girls invited to social at A.B.G.S. [Ashby Boys' Grammar School.]

Saturday August 21st

All worked for 1 hour only owing to rain at Packington.

P Best, S Marlow & A Sabine stayed behind.

E Daws, M Jackson, E Nelson, J Preston, M Jones
D Elvey employed by farmer for stooking.

Ashby de la Zouch Girls' Wartime Harvest Camps 1942-1944

Log. August 21-28. 1943

Sat: Aug 21 Miss Bayford took over for Sat. a.m., Miss Baker at 2pm along with Miss Morton & Miss Wilkinson (Stafford). 18 girls in residence. B. Mercer & E. Davis went to Burton, B. Fryer & D. Johnson to Loughborough (taxi back from Coalville). The rest were free until supper time.
Morning & evening prayers & roll call decided upon.

Sun: Aug 22 8 girls went to early service (4 Stafford, 4 Ashby (Erdington)). Most of the rest went to later services.
p.m. 4 Stafford girls & P. Driscoll set out cycling to Charnwood Forest. At Ravenstone had puncture, so returned home. The other girls returned. Total in residence 43 girls, 4 staff.

Mon: 23rd All at Packington. Supervision: a.m. Miss Wilkinson p.m. Miss Morton. Half the party cycled, rest went by Hipwell's bus – leaving Market St. 8.45 the field at 4p [fare 2d]
J. Reece not very well returned with Miss Wilkinson on 1.20 bus, but up again for dinner.
5.30 Party of girls kindly shown over Church by Canon Hanford Evening – tennis on all courts with boy campers as visitors. The Boys' Harvest Camp had entertained the girls on 2 evenings last week & the girls had asked permission

Saturday August 21st
Miss Bayford took over from Saturday a.m., Miss Baker at 2pm
along with Miss Morton and Miss Wilkinson (Stafford).
18 girls in residence. B Mercer and E Davis went to Burton,
B Fryer and D Johnson to Loughborough (taxi back from Coalville).
The rest were free until suppertime.

Morning and evening prayers and roll call decided upon.

Sunday August 22nd
8 girls went to early service (4 Stafford, 4 Ashby (Erdington)).
Most of the rest went to later services.
p.m. 4 Stafford girls and P Driscoll set out cycling to Charnwood Forest. At Ravenstone had puncture so returned home. The other girls returned.
Total in residence 43 girls, 4 staff.

Monday August 23
All at Packington. Supervision am Miss Wilkinson, pm Miss Morton.
Half the party cycled, rest went by Hipwell's Bus, leaving Market Street 8.45 and the field at 4 (Fare 2d)

J Reece not very well, returned with Miss Wilkinson on 1.20 bus but up again for dinner.

5.30 party of girls kindly shown over Church by Canon Hanford.
Evening – tennis in all courts with boy campers as visitors.
The Boys' Harvest Camp had entertained the girls on 2 evenings last week and the girls has asked permission [continued on next page]

Ashby de la Zouch Girls' Wartime Harvest Camps 1942-1944

to give a return party. They were told to choose an entertainments committee, prepare a programme & submit it. After discussion of it with them, it was decided they might give it & the invitation for 45 boys was communicated (3d subscription for refreshments)

Tues. Aug 24 All at Packington 9-2 Miss Norton 2-4 Misses Bayford & Wilkinson. No incidents in the field.
8-10 The Party. dancing & games in Dining Room using gramophone. Refreshments disappeared as if by magic – buns (Mr Thorley had made 144 & some were bought), biscuits, lemonade, cold coffee, hot cocoa.
Stunts by Croydon boys & community singing in room 16. Auld Lang Syne at 10. Behaviour very good.
Lights out at 10.30.

Wed. Aug 25 All at Packington. 9-1.15 Miss Baker. 12-3.30 Miss Norton 2-4 Miss Bayford & Miss Wilkinson.
Evening. Seniors went to film show "Ask a Policeman" at Boys' Grammar School. Juniors shown pictures through epidiascope of Ashby & last year's Harvest Camp. Tennis & dancing for others.

[continued from previous page] to give a return party. They were told to choose an entertainments committee, prepare a programme, submit it. After discussion of it with them, it was decided they might give it and the invitation for 45 boys was communicated. (3d subscription for refreshments)

Tuesday 24th August
All at Packington 9 – 2. Miss Morton 2 – 4 Misses Bayford & Wilkinson.

No incidents on the field.

8 – 10 the party, dancing and games in the Dining Room using gramophone. Refreshments disappeared as if by magic - buns (Mrs Thorley had made 144 and some were bought), biscuits, lemonade, cold coffee, hot cocoa.

Stunts by Croydon boys and community singing in room 16.
Auld Lang Syne at 10.
Behaviour very good. Lights out at 10.30.

Wednesday August 25th
All at Packington 9 – 1.15. Miss Baker 12 – 3.30 Miss Morton, 2 – 4 Miss Bayford and Miss Wilkinson.

Evening, seniors went to film show "Ask a Policeman" at Boys' Grammar School. Juniors shown pictures through epidiascope of Ashby & last year's harvest camp.

Tennis and dancing for others.

Ashby de la Zouch Girls' Wartime Harvest Camps 1942-1944

Midnight. Staff & girls disturbed by 'marauders' on the lawn - boys from H.C. [Incident reported to Miss Champion & Mathon]

Thurs: Aug 26 All at Packington 9-1.15 Miss Wilkinson, 12-3 Miss Morton, 2-4 Miss Bayford. With the help of about 20 girls from Coalville Grammar School, & 10 land girls the 9-acre field was pulled, only the thistles left standing. Evening - Juniors to film show at Boys' School, Picture show repeated for Seniors.
Letter received from Miss Whitehurst, saying she would prefer that all the Stafford girls travelled home with their staff on Saturday, so M. Reynolds & J. Brown will not be staying next week.

Fri: Aug 27 Stookers set off in spite of rain & completed work at Packington in 1 hr, returning in time to set off with the rest to Ottewell Farm Nottingham Rd. (35-40 mins walk) as soon as instructors arrived. Supervisors: with cyclists Miss Morton, with walkers Misses Bates & Wilkinson
After tea, several girls were given permission to visit the Castle.

Sat: Aug 28 Heavy rain - no outdoor work. Girls packed, tidied their rooms, piled up mattresses & blankets, & amused themselves. Maclean's taxi ordered for 2.30, for Stafford luggage for 3.12 train

Midnight, staff and girls disturbed by "marauders" on the lawn – boys from H. C. [Harvst Camp] (Incident reported to Miss Champion and Mr Matthews).

Thursday August 26th
All at Packington 9 – 1.15, Miss Wilkinson, 12-3 Miss Morton, 2 – 4 Miss Bayford.
With the help of about 20 girls from Coalville Grammar School and 10 land girls, the 9 acre field was pulled, only the thistles left standing.

Evening – juniors to film show at Boys' School. Picture show repeated for seniors.

Letter received from Miss Whitehurst saying she would prefer that all the Stafford girls travelled home with their staff on Saturday, so M Reynolds and J Brown will not be staying next week.

Friday August 27th
Stookers set off in spite of rain, completed work at Packington in 1 hr returning in time to set off with the rest to Ottewell Farm, Nottingham Road (35 – 40 minutes walk) as soon as instructions arrived.

Supervisors with cyclists Miss Morton, with walkers Misses Baker and Wilkinson.

After tea, several girls were given permission to visit the Castle.

Saturday August 28th
Heavy rain – no outdoor work. Girls packed, tidied their rooms, piled up mattresses and blankets and amused themselves.

Machin's taxi ordered for 2.30 for Stafford luggage for 3.12 train.

Ashby de la Zouch Girls' Wartime Harvest Camps 1942-1944

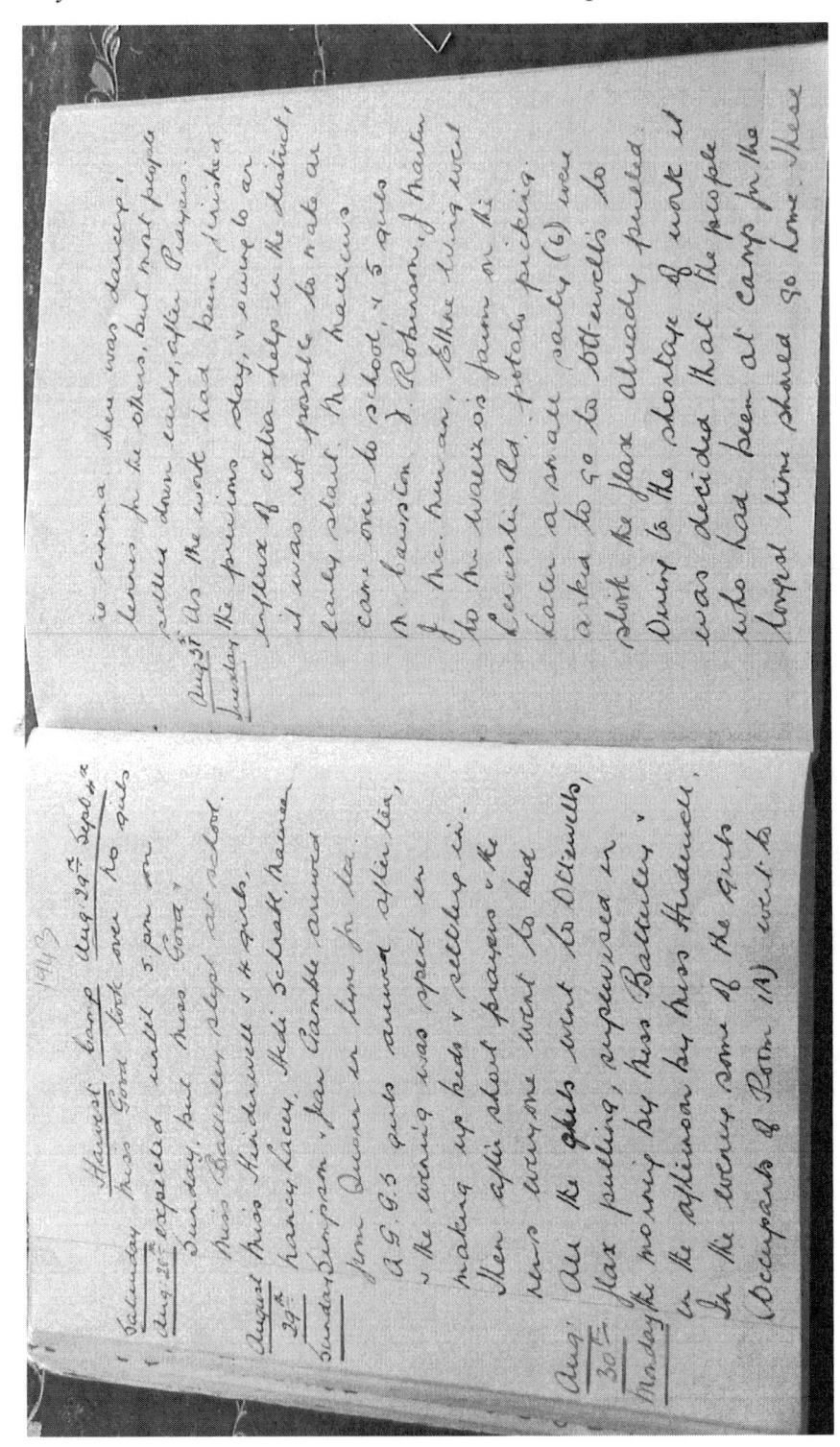

Wendy Freer

Harvest Camp August 29th – Sept 4th

Saturday 28th August

Miss Good took over. No girls expected until 5pm on Sunday but Miss Good and Miss Batterley slept at school.

Sunday 29th August

Miss Hinderwell and 4 girls, Nancy Lacey, Heidi Schnell, Maureen Simpson, & Jean Gamble arrived from Quorn in time for tea.

A.G.S.G (Ashby Girls Grammar School girls) arrived after tea, and the evening was spent in making up beds and settling in. Then after short prayers and the news, everyone went to bed.

Monday 30th August

All the girls went to Ottewells, flax pulling, supervised in the morning by Miss Batterley, in the afternoon by Miss Hindwell.

In the evening some of the girls (occupants of Room 1A) went to the cinema. There was dancing and tennis for the others but most people settled down early after prayers.

Tuesday 31st August

As the work had been finished the previous day, and owing to an influx of extra help in the district, it was not possible to make an early start.

Mr Matthews came over to the school and 5 girls, (M Cawston, D Robinson, J Martin, J McMuran, Ethne Wing) went to Mr Walter's farm on the Leicester Road, potato picking.

Later a small party (6) were asked to go to Ottewells to stook the flax already pulled. Owing to the shortage of work it was decided that the people who had been at camp for the longest time should go home. These

[continued on next page]

Ashby de la Zouch Girls' Wartime Harvest Camps 1942-1944

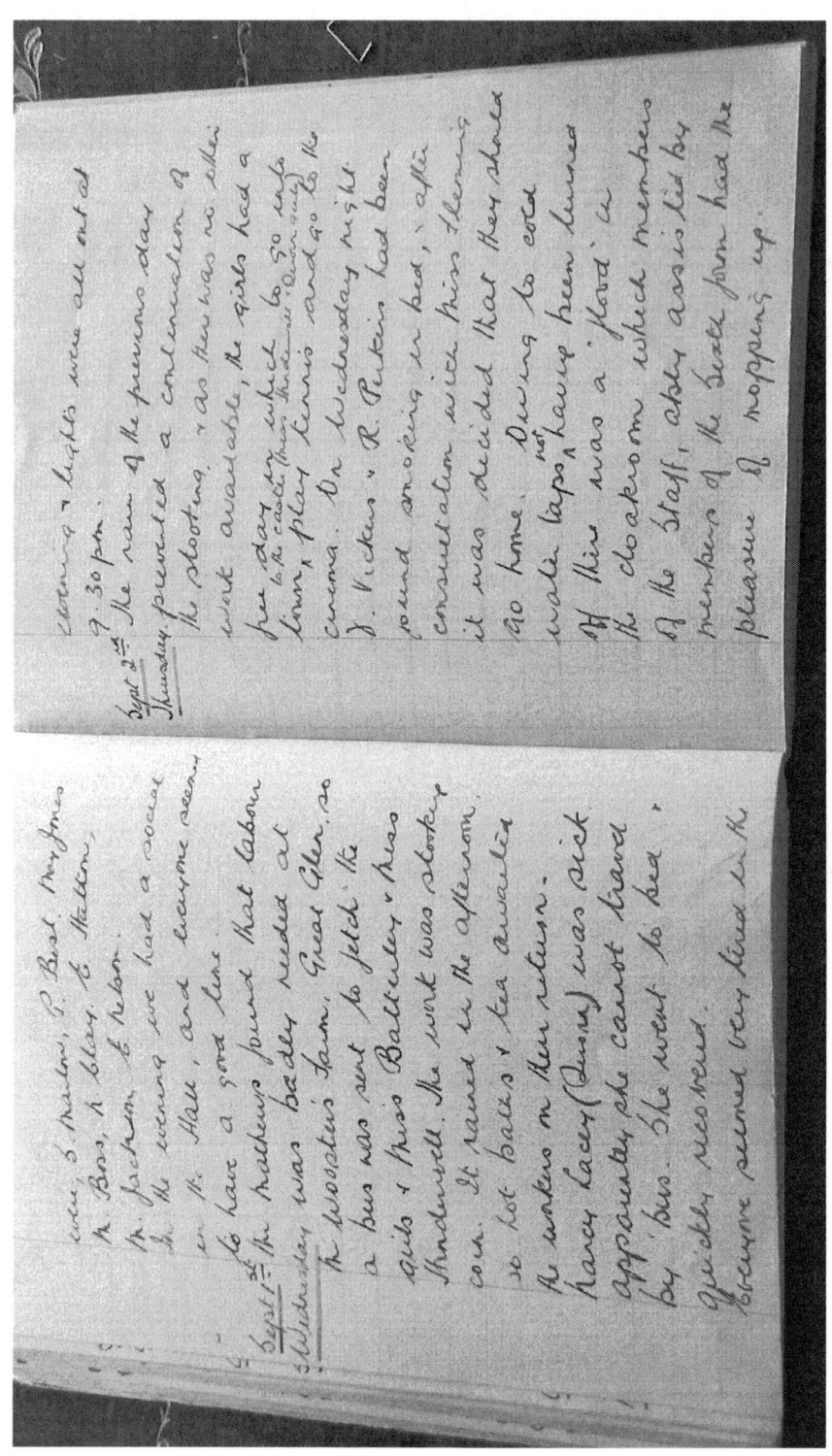

[continued from previous page]
were S Marlow, P Best, Margaret Jones, M Boss, N Clay, E Hatton, M Jackson, E Nelson.

In the evening, we had a social in the Hall and everyone seemed to have a good time.

Wednesday 1st September

Mr Matthews found that labour was badly needed at Wooster's farm, Great Glen, so a bus was sent to fetch the girls and Miss Batterley and Miss Hindwell. The work was stooking corn. It rained in the afternoon, so hot baths and tea awaited the workers on their return. Nancy Lacey (Quorn) was sick. Apparently she cannot travel by bus. She went to bed and quickly recovered.

Everyone seemed very tired in the evening and lights were all out by 9.30pm.

Thursday 2nd September

The rain of the previous day prevented a continuation of the stooking and as there was no work available, the girls had a free day in which to go into town, to the castle (Miss Hinerwell and Quorn girls) play tennis and go to the cinema. On Wednesday night, D Vickers & R Perkins had been found smoking in bed. After consultation with Miss Fleming it was decided that they should go home.

Owing to cold water taps not having been turned off, there was a "flood" in the cloakroom which members of the staff, ably assisted by members of the sixth form, had the pleasure of mopping up.

Friday 3rd September

News was received that labour was needed at the War Agricultural Committee's farm at Glenfield so 29 girls, Miss Kesterton, Miss Hinderwell and 10 boys from the A.B.G.S. (Ashby Boys' Grammar School) went by bus (N Lacey left at school). The work was pulling cabbages.

In the evening Mr Matthews invited us all over for a social and everyone really enjoyed themselves and made a night of it, as it was the end of this year's camp.

Saturday 4th September

Blankets and mattresses stacked by 10.15.

Wendy Freer

4 Ashby Girls' Wartime Harvest Camp 1944

In the final year of the camps recorded in the log, the numbers of girls attending had vastly expanded. On Tuesday, 1st August, 81 girls were in residence; 14 arrived from Stafford, 27 from Kidderminster and 19 from Erdington. In addition, there was an unspecified number of Ashby girls in residence.

No roll call or accounts are contained in the logbook for 1944. Perhaps the large numbers necessitated a separate record being kept. It would appear that the boys' camp was also very large as, on one occasion, 60 boys arrived at the girls' camp to take part in a social evening.

The first camp lasted two weeks with girls departing early on Tuesday 14th August. Later the same day, 20 girls arrived from Erdington and 14 from Stafford for the second two-week camp of the summer. Again, Ashby girls also took part.

1944 was the year in which one of the teachers taking part in the first two-week camp took it upon herself to keep a more detailed diary and illustrate it with pencil drawings which really help to bring the story to life. The colleague who followed her also wrote in a fair amount of detail but there are no illustrations. However, a mysterious occurrence in the middle of the last night remained unexplained when the girls departed the next morning. One has to suspect that the boys' camp had something to do with it!

The log ends on Tuesday 22nd August but the notes on accidents and ailments suggests that the camp actually continued until at least 10th September.

This accident and ailment page is a new addition which did not appear in previous years, unless it was recorded in a separate book. It shows girls suffering from the effects of hard work in the field, often in wet conditions, although, how Sheila Chambers managed to cut her head on a lemonade bottle remains a mystery!

Ashby de la Zouch Girls' Wartime Harvest Camps 1942-1944

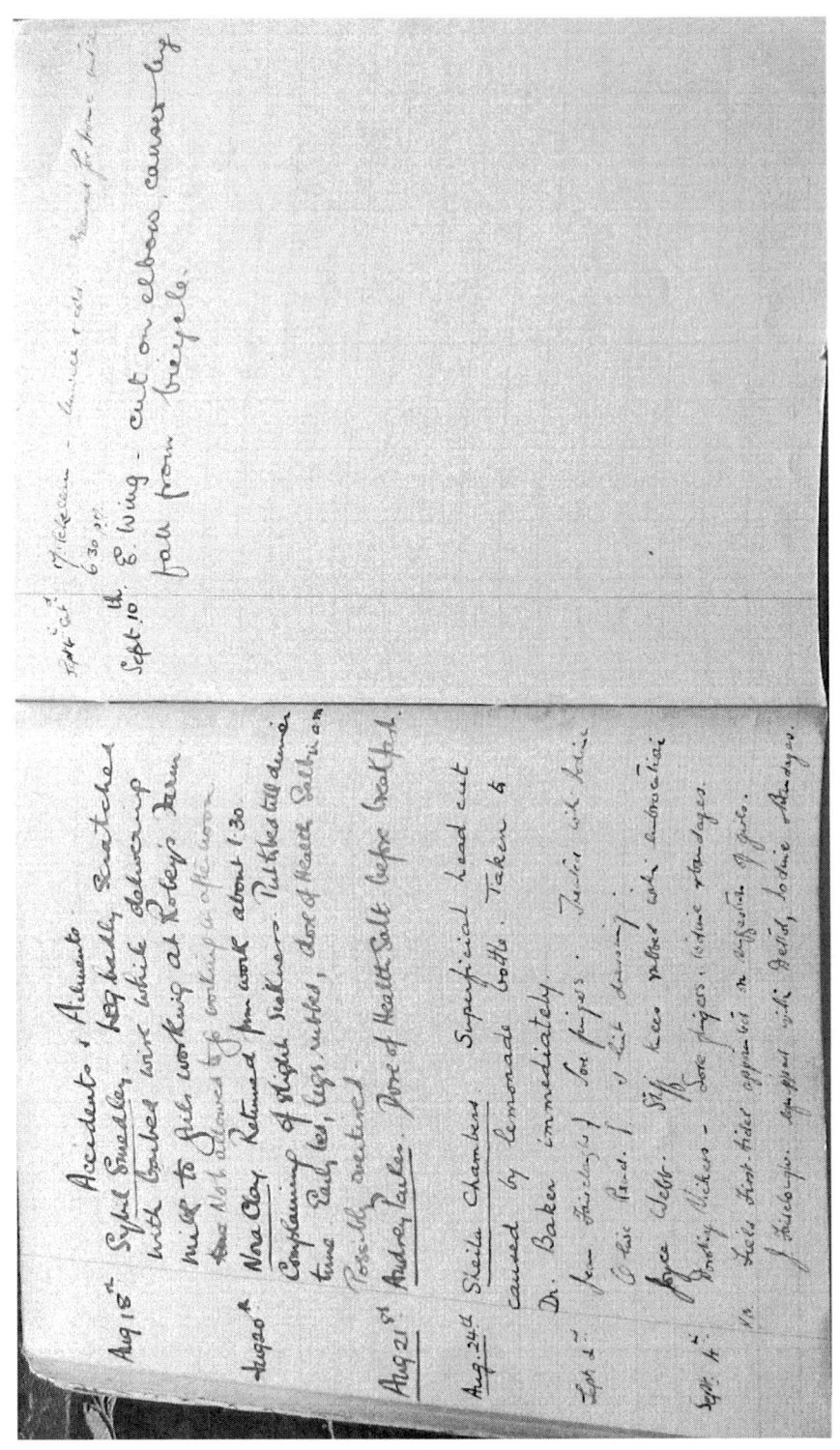

Accidents and Ailments

August 18th
Sybil Smedley leg badly scratched with barbed wire while delivering milk to girls working at Robey's Farm.
Not allowed to go working in afternoon.

August 20th
Nora Clay returned from work about 1.30. Complaining of slight sickness. Put to bed till dinner time. Early bed, legs rubbed, dose of Health Salts in am. Probably overtired.

August 21st
Audrey Parker Dose of Health Salt before breakfast.

August 24th
Sheila Chambers Superficial head cut caused by lemonade bottle. Taken to Dr Baker immediately.

Sept 2nd
Jean Fairclough: sore fingers treated with iodine
Olive Read: a lint dressing
Joyce Webb: stiff knees rubbed with embrocation

Sept 4th
Dorothy Vickers – sore fingers, iodine and bandages

N.B. Field First-aider appointed on suggestion of girls.
J Fairclough equipped with Dettol, iodine and bandages.

Sept 4th cont.
M McLellan unwell + cold. Excused for home until 6.30pm.

Sept 10th
E Wing – cut on elbow caused by fall from bicycle.

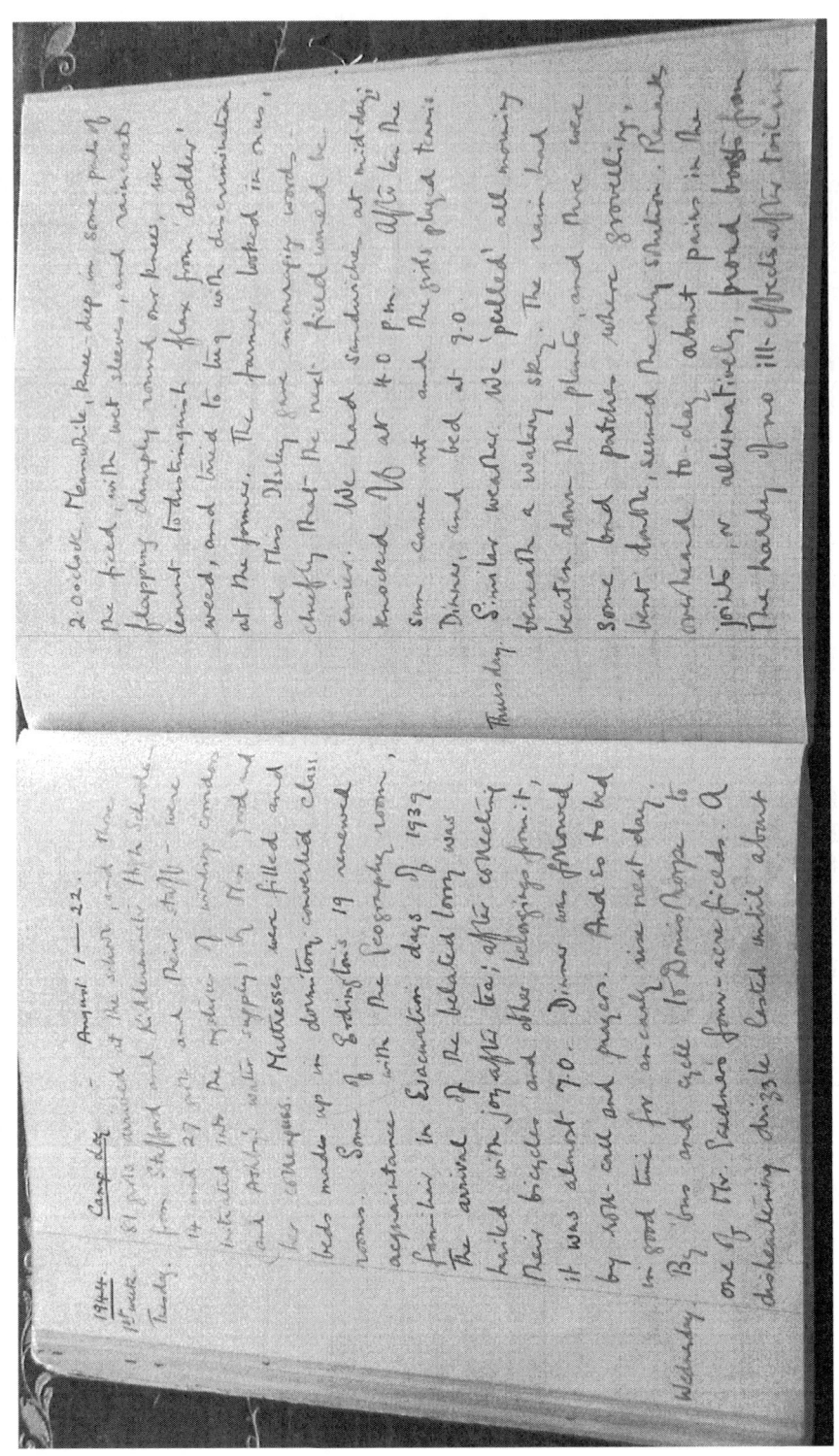

Camp log August 1st – 22nd

Tuesday 1st August

81 girls arrived at the school and those from Stafford and Kidderminster High School – 14 and 27 girls and their staff – were initiated into the mysteries of winding corridors and Ashby's water supply by Miss Good and her colleagues. Mattresses were filled [with straw] and beds made up in the dormitory converted classrooms. Some of Erdington's 19 renewed acquaintance with the geography room, familiar in evacuation days of 1939. The arrival of the belated lorry was hailed with joy after tea; after collecting their bicycles and their belongings from it, it was almost 7.0. Dinner was followed by roll call and prayers. And so to bed in good time for an early rise the next day.

Wednesday 2nd August

By bus and cycle to Donisthorpe to one of Mr Gardener's four acre fields. A disheartening drizzle lasted until about 2 o clock. Meanwhile, knee deep in some parts of the field, with wet sleeves and raincoats flapping damply round our knees, we learnt to distinguish flax from "dodder" weed and tried to tug with discernment at the former. The farmer looked in and Miss Ilsley gave encouraging words, chiefly that the next field would be easier. We had sandwiches at midday and knocked off at 4pm. After tea the sun came out and the girls played tennis. Dinner, and bed at 9.0.

Thursday 3rd August

Similar weather. We "pulled" all morning beneath a watery sky. The rain had beaten the plants and there were some bad patches where grovelling, bent double, seemed the only solution. Remarks overheard today about pains in joints, or alternatively proud boasts from the hardy of no ill effects after toiling [continued on next page]

Ashby de la Zouch Girls' Wartime Harvest Camps 1942-1944

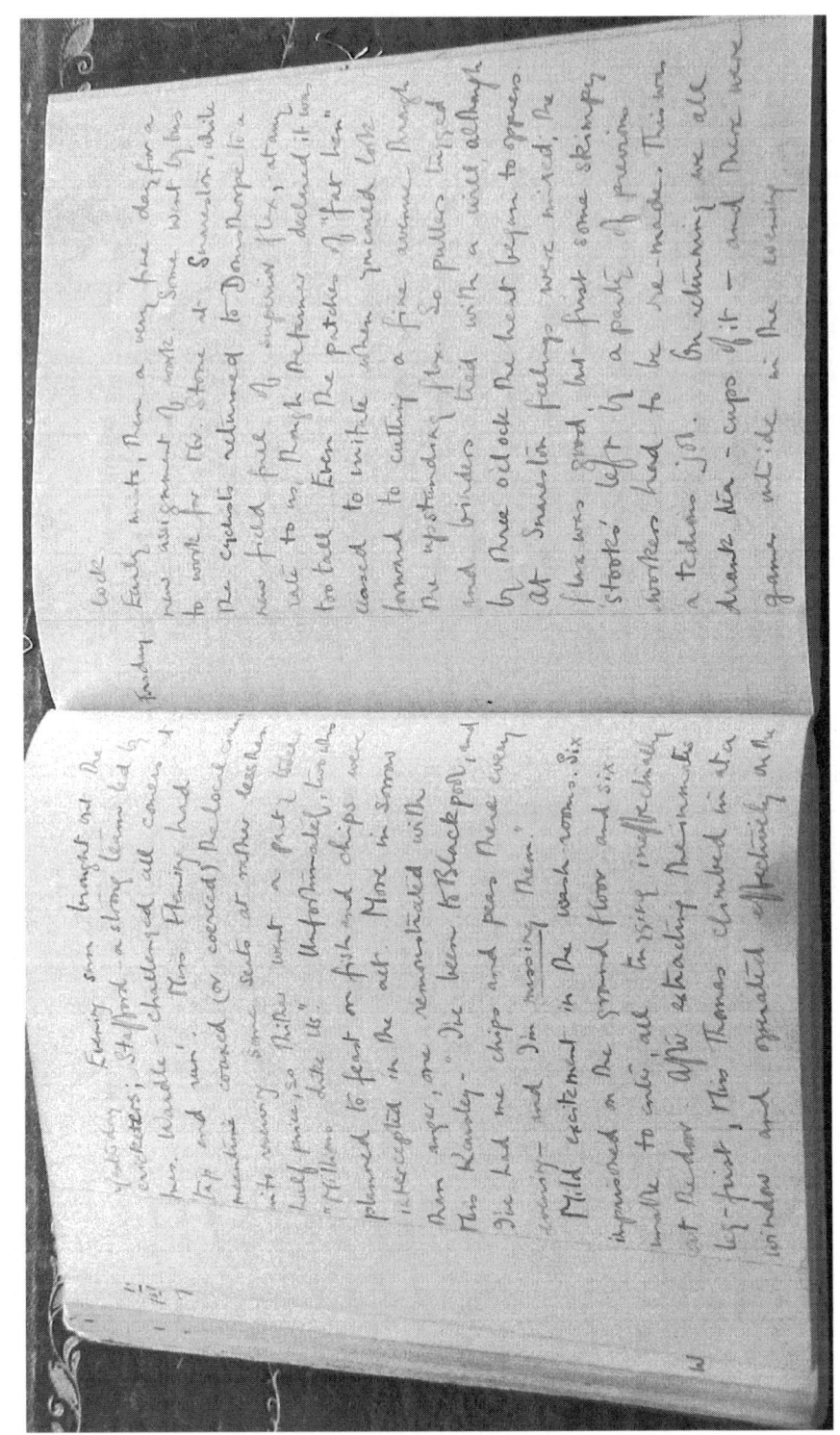

[continued from previous page] yesterday. Evening sun brought out the cricketers; Stafford, a strong team led by Miss Wardle, challenged all comers at "tip and run". Miss Fleming had meantime coaxed (or coerced) the local cinema into reserving some seats at rather less than half price so thither went a party to see "Millions Like Us". Unfortunately, two who planned to feast on fish and chips were intercepted in the act. More in sorrow than in anger, one remonstrated with Miss Kearsley – "I've been to Blackpool and I've had me chips and peas there every evening and I'm *missing* them."

Mild excitement in the washrooms. Six imprisoned on the ground floor and six unable to enter, all tugging ineffectually at the door. After extracting the inmates, leg first, Miss Thomas climbed in at a window and operated effectively on the lock.

Friday 4th August 1944

Early mists and then a very fine day for an early assignment of work. Some went by bus to work for Mr Stone at Snareston, while the cyclists returned to Donisthorpe to a new field full of superior flax, - at any rate to us, though the farmer declared it was too tall. Even the patches of "fat hen" ceased to irritate when you could look forward to cutting a fine avenue through the upstanding flax. So pullers tugged and binders tied with a will, although by three o clock the heat began to oppress. At Snareston feelings were mixed; the flax was good, but first some skimpy stooks left by a party of pervious workers had to be remade. This was a tedious job. On returning, we all drank tea – cups of it – and there were games outside in the evening.

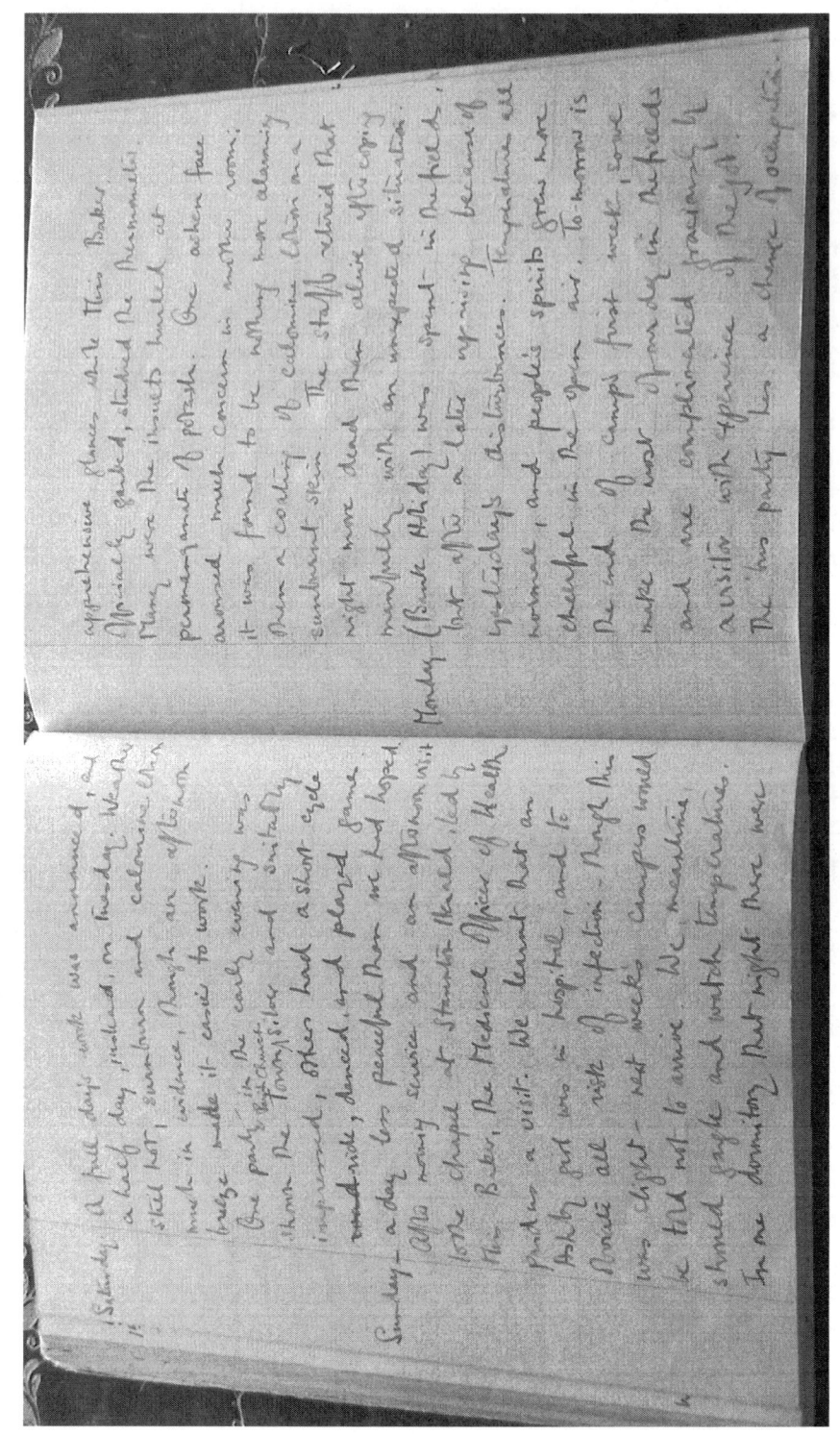

Saturday 5th August

A full day's work was announced and a half day instead on Tuesday. Weather still hot, sunburn and calamine lotion much in evidence, though an afternoon breeze made it easier to work.

One party in the early evening was shown the Town Parish Church silver and suitably impressed, others had a short cycle ride, danced and played games.

Sunday 6th August

A day less peaceful than we had hoped. After morning service, and an afternoon visit to the chapel at Staunton Harold, led by Miss Baker, the Medical Officer of Health paid us a visit. We learnt that an Ashby girl was in hospital, and to obviate all risk of infection, though this was slight, next week's campers would be told not to arrive. We, meantime, should gargle and watch temperatures. In one dormitory that night there were apprehensive glances while Miss Baker officially gargled, studied the thermometer. Many were the insults hurled at permanganate of potash. One ashen face aroused much concern in another room; it was found to be nothing more alarming than a coating of calamine lotion on sunburnt skin. The staff retired that night more dead than alive after coping manfully with an unexpected situation.

Monday (Bank Holiday) 7th August

was spent in the field but after a later uprising because of yesterday's disturbances. Temperatures all normal, and people's spirits grew more cheerful in the open air. Tomorrow is the end of camp's first week, so we make the most of the day in the fields and are complimented graciously by a visitor with experience of the job. The bus party has a change of occupation.

[continued on next page]

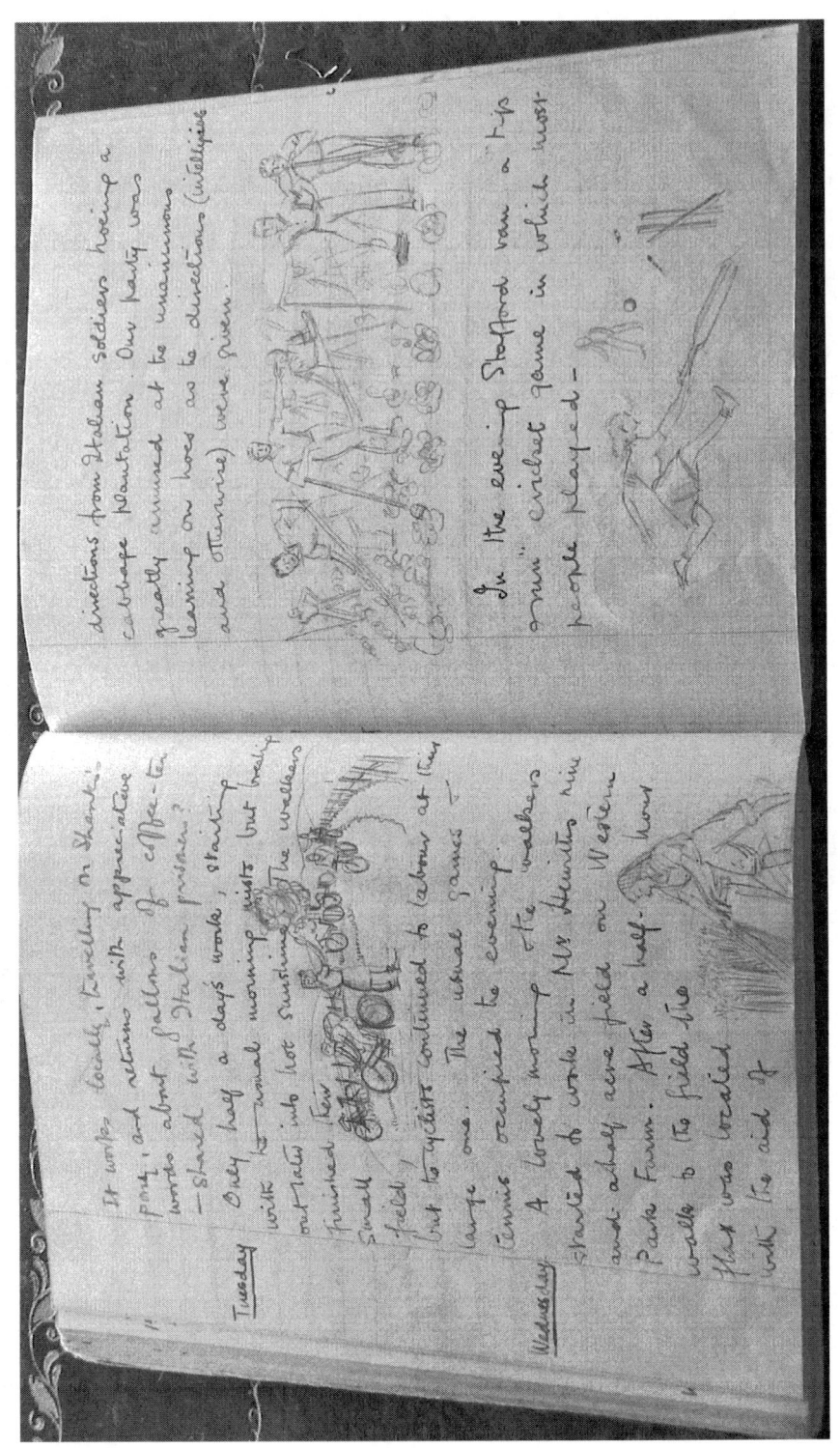

[continued from previous page] It works locally, travelling on Shanks's pony and returns with appreciative words about gallons of coffee – tea – shared with Italian prisoners?

Tuesday 8th August

Only half a day's work, starting with the usual morning mists but breaking out later into hot sunshine.

The walkers finished their small field, but the cyclists continued to labour at their large one. The usual games of tennis occupied the evening.

Wednesday 9th August

A lovely morning and the walkers started to work in Mr Hewitt's nine and a half acre field on Western Park Farm. After a half hour walk to the field, the flax was located with the aid of directions from Italian soldiers hoeing a cabbage plantation. Our party was greatly amused at the unanimous leaning on hoes as the directions (intelligible and otherwise) were given.

In the evening Stafford ran a "tip and run" cricket game in which most people played.

Italian prisoners of war, "unanimously" leaning on their hoes

The cyclists go off to continue their labour

Pulling flax

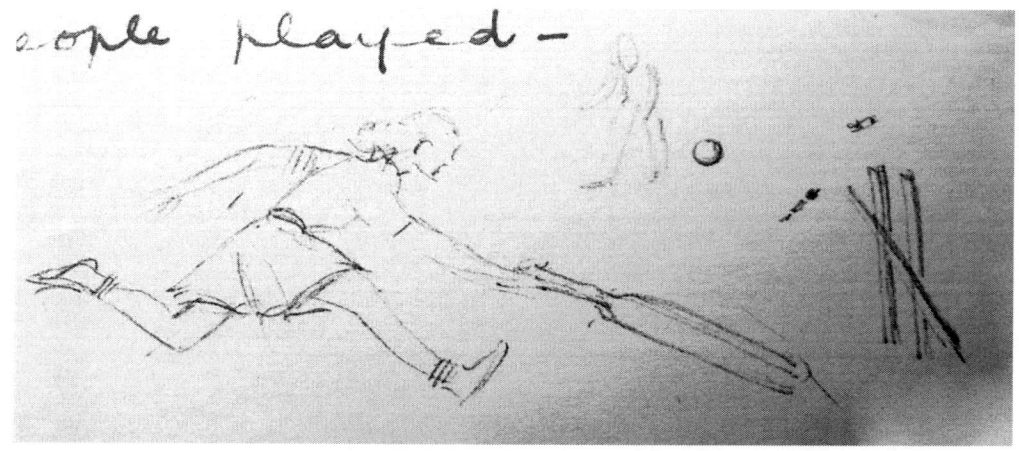

The cricket match in which most people played

Ashby de la Zouch Girls' Wartime Harvest Camps 1942-1944

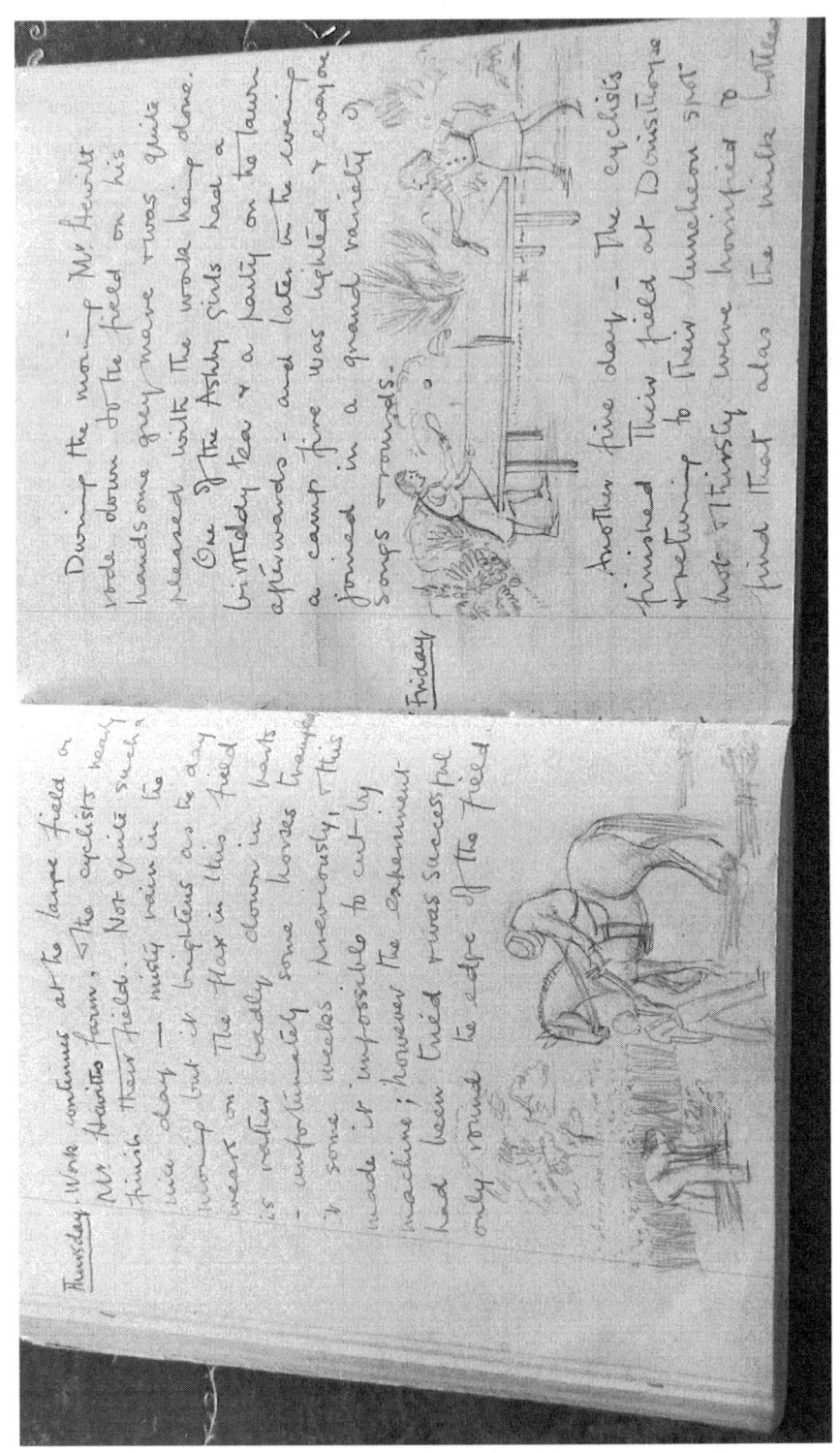

Thursday 10th August

Work continues at the large field on Mr Hewitt's farm, the cyclists nearly finish their field. Not quite such a nice day – misty rain in the morning but it brightens as the day wears on. The flax in this field is rather badly trampled down in parts as unfortunately some horses trampled it some weeks previously and this made it impossible to cut by machine; however the experiment had been tried and was successful only round the edge of the field.

During the morning, Mr Hewitt rode down to the field on his handsome grey mare and was quite pleased with the work being done.

One of the Ashby girls had a birthday tea and a party on the lawn afterwards – and later in the evening a camp fire was lighted and everyone joined in a grand variety of songs and rounds.

Friday 11th August

Another fine day – The cyclists finished their field at Donisthorpe and returning to their luncheon spot hot and thirsty were horrified to find that alas the milk bottles [continued on page 57]

Ashby de la Zouch Girls' Wartime Harvest Camps 1942-1944

Farmer, Mr Hewitt, rides down to inspect the work

After work, the girls still have the energy to play table tennis!

Ashby de la Zouch Girls' Wartime Harvest Camps 1942-1944

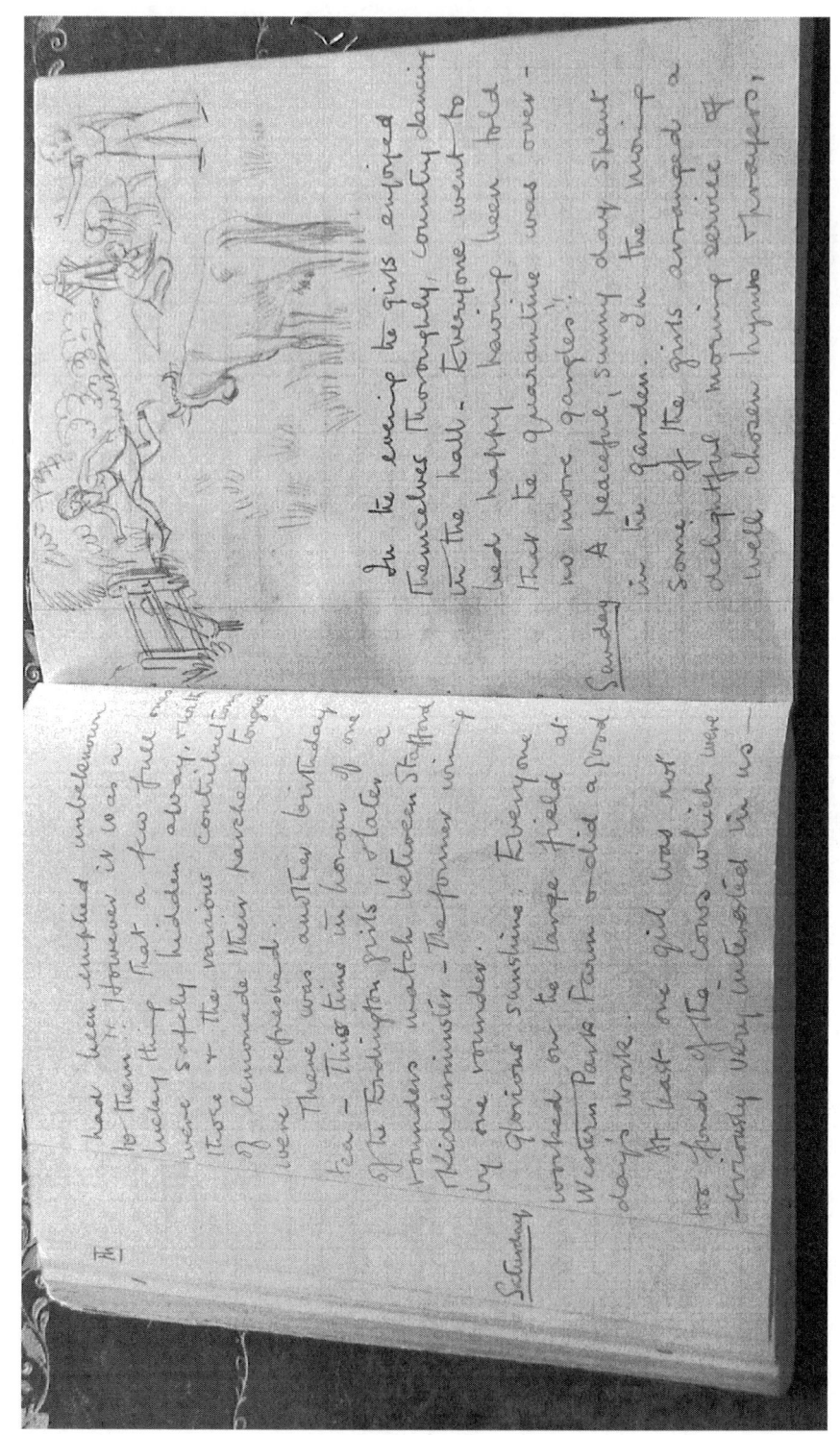

[continued from page 53] had been emptied unbeknown to them!! However, it was a lucky thing that a few full ones were safely hidden away and with those, and the various contributions of lemonade, their parched tongues were refreshed.

There was another birthday tea – this time in honour of one of the Erdington girls, later a rounders match between Stafford and Kidderminster – the former winning by one rounder.

Saturday 12th August

Glorious sunshine. Everyone worked on the large field at Western Park Farm and did a good day's work. At least one girl was not too fond of the cows which were obviously very interested in us.

In the evening the girls enjoyed themselves thoroughly, country dancing in the hall. Everyone went to bed happy having been told that the quarantine was over – no more gargles!

Sunday 12th August

A peaceful sunny day spent in the garden. In the morning some of the girls arranged a delightful morning service of well chosen hymns and prayers [continued on next page]

The girl who wasn't too fond of cows!

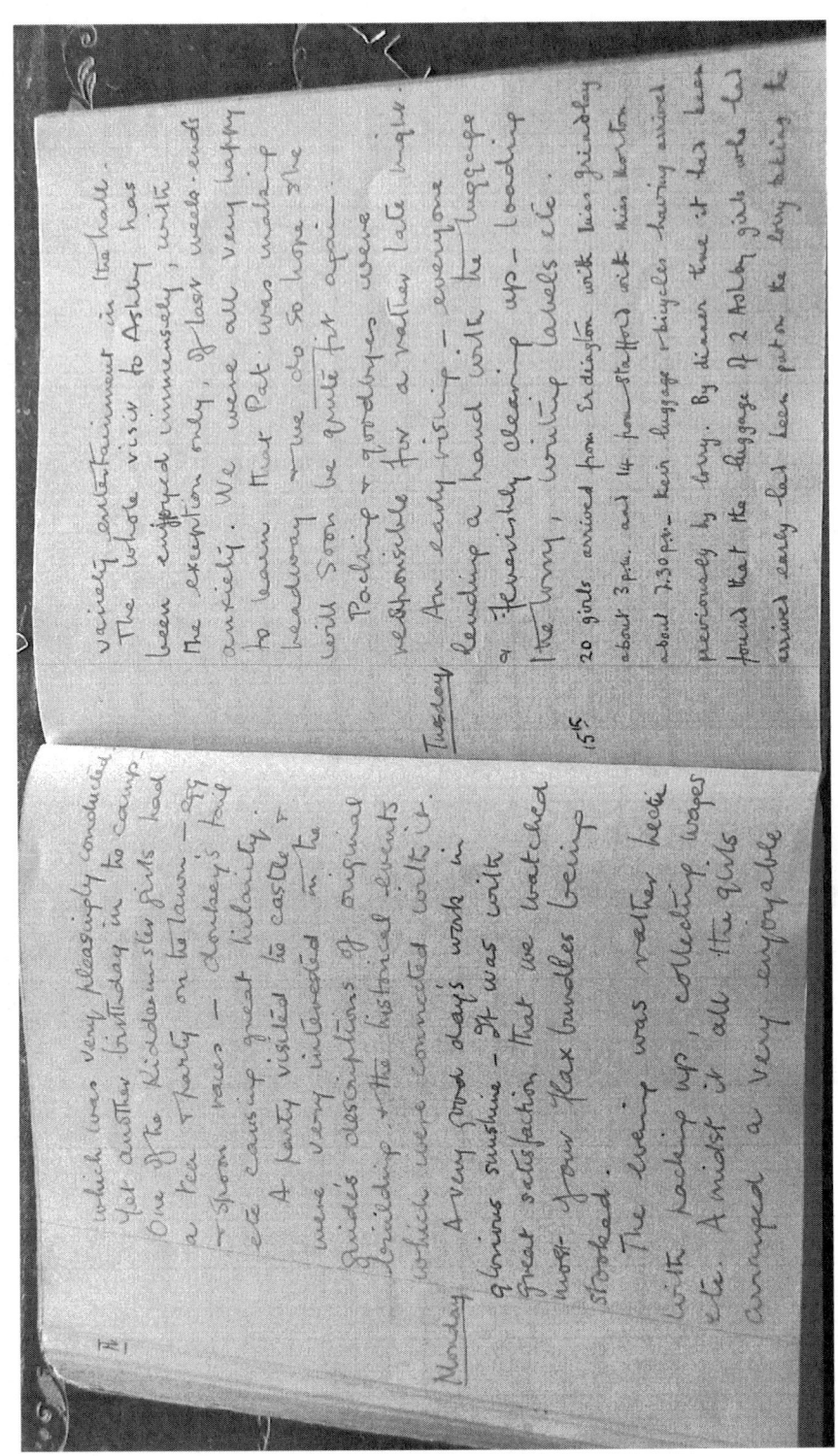

which was very pleasingly conducted yet another birthday in to camp. One of the Kidderminster girls had a tea Party on to lawn — 999 — from ours — Lindsey's hat is causing great hilarity. A party visited to castle & were very interested in the guide's descriptions of original building & the historical events which were connected with it.

Monday A very good day's work in glorious sunshine. It was with great satisfaction that we watched most of our flax bundles being stooked.

The evening was rather hectic with packing up, collecting wages etc. A midst it all the girls arranged a very enjoyable variety entertainment in the hall. The whole visit to Ashby has been enjoyed immensely, with the exception only of Joan's week-ends anxiety. We were all very happy to learn that Pat was making headway & we do so hope she will soon be quite fit again. Packing & goodbyes were responsible for a rather late [night?].

Tuesday An early rising — everyone lending a hand with the luggage & feverishly cleaning up — loading the lorry, writing labels etc.

15th 20 girls arrived from Sudington with Miss Grindley about 3pm and 14 from Stafford with Miss Knutton about 7.30 pm — their luggage & bicycles having arrived previously by lorry. By dinner time it had been found that the luggage of 2 Ashby girls who had arrived early had been put on to lorry taking to

which was very pleasingly conducted. Yet another birthday in the camp. One of the Kidderminster girls had a tea and party on the lawn – egg and spoon races – donkey's tail etc causing great hilarity.

A party visited the castle and were very interested in the guide's descriptions of original building and the historical events which were connected with it.

Monday 13th August

A very good day's work in glorious sunshine – It was with great satisfaction that we watched most of our flax bundles being stooked.

The evening was rather hectic with packing up, collecting wages etc. Amidst it all the girls arranged a very enjoyable variety entertainment in the hall. The whole visit to Ashby has been enjoyed immensely, with the exception only of the last week-end's anxiety. We were all very happy to learn that Pat was making headway and we do so hope she will soon be quite fit again.

Packing and goodbyes were responsible for a rather late night.

Tuesday 14th August

An early rising – everyone lending a hand with the luggage and feverishly clearing up – loading the lorry, writing labels etc.

[Here the handwriting changes, indicating another teacher taking over]

20 girls arrive from Erdington with Miss Grindlay about 3 pm and 14 from Stafford with Miss Horton about 7.30pm. their luggage and bicycles having arrived previously by lorry. By dinner time it had been found that the luggage of 2 Ashby girls who had arrived early had been put on the lorry taking the [continued on next page]

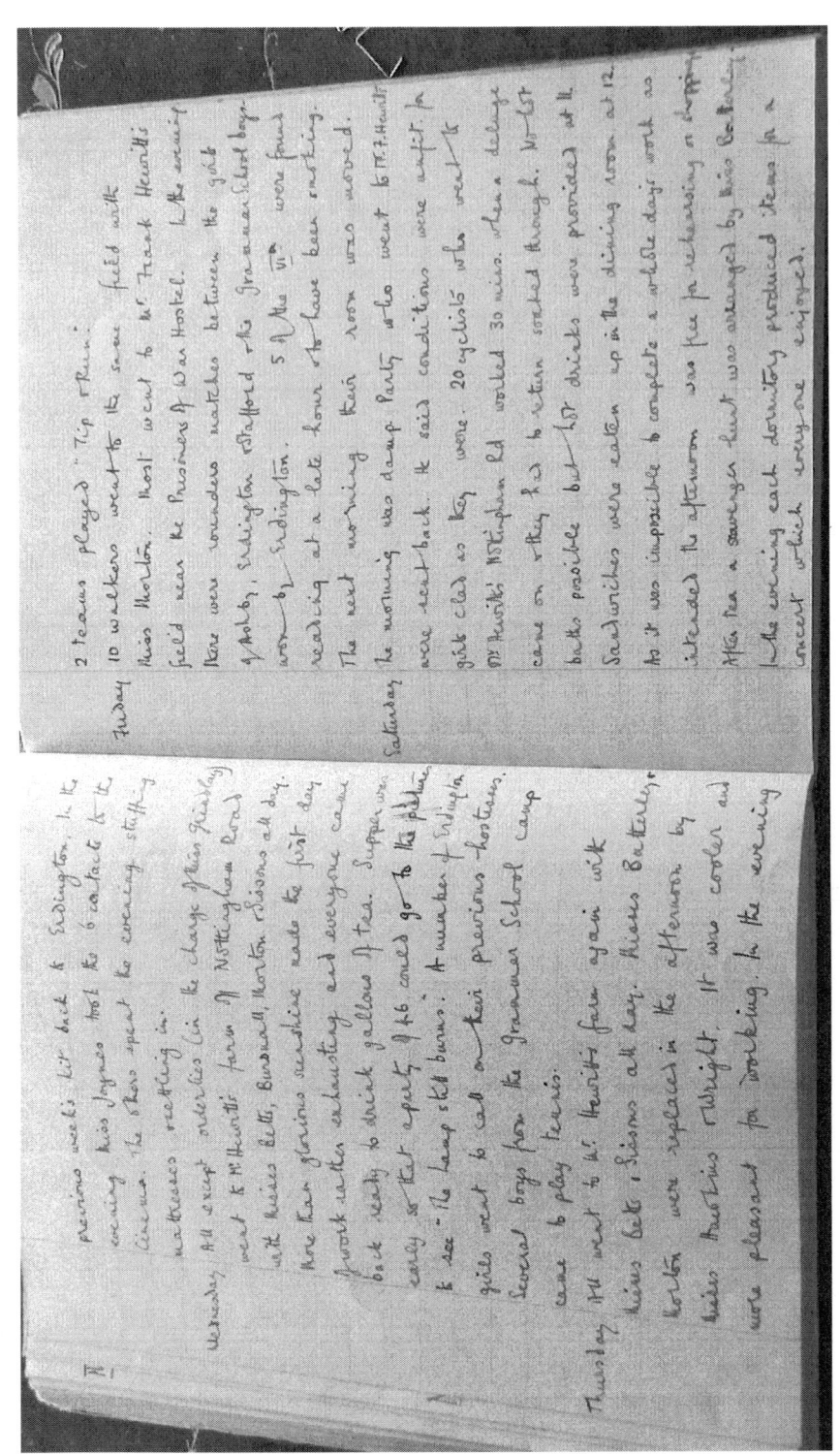

[continued from previous page] previous week's kit back to Erdington. In the evening, Miss Joynes took the 6 contacts to the cinema. The others spent the evening stuffing mattresses and settling in.

Wednesday 15th August

All except orderlies (in the charge of Miss Grindlay) went to Mr Hewitt's farm off Nottingham Road with Misses Betts, Bursnall, Morton, Sissons all day. More than glorious sunshine made the first day of work rather exhausting and everyone came back ready to drink gallons of tea. Supper was early so that a party of 46 could go to the pictures to see *"The Lamp Still Burns"*. A number of the Erdington girls went to call on their previous hostesses. Several boys from the Grammar School camp came to play tennis.

Thursday 16th August

All went to Mr Hewitt's farm again with Misses Betts and Sissons all day. Misses Batterley and Morton were replaced in the afternoon by Misses Hawkins and Wright. It was cooler and more pleasant for working. In the evening, 2 teams played "Tip and Run".

Friday 17th August

Walkers went to the same field with Miss Horton. Most went to Mr Frank Hewitt's field near the Prisoners of War Hostel. In the evening there were rounders matches between the girls of Ashby, Erdington and Stafford and the Grammar School boys, won by Erdington. 5 of the VIth were found reading at a late hour and to have been smoking. The next morning their room was moved.

Saturday 18th August

The morning was damp. Party who went to Mr Hewitt were sent back. He said conditions were unfit for girls clad as they were. 20 cyclists who went to Mr Hewitt's Nottingham Road worked 30 minutes when a deluge came on and they had to return, soaked through. No hot baths possible but hot drinks were provided at 11. Sandwiches were eaten up in the dining room at 12. As it was impossible to complete a whole day's work as intended, the afternoon was free for rehearsing or shopping. After tea, a scavenger hunt was arranged by Miss Batterley. In the evening, each dormitory produced items for a concert which everyone enjoyed.

Ashby de la Zouch Girls' Wartime Harvest Camps 1942-1944

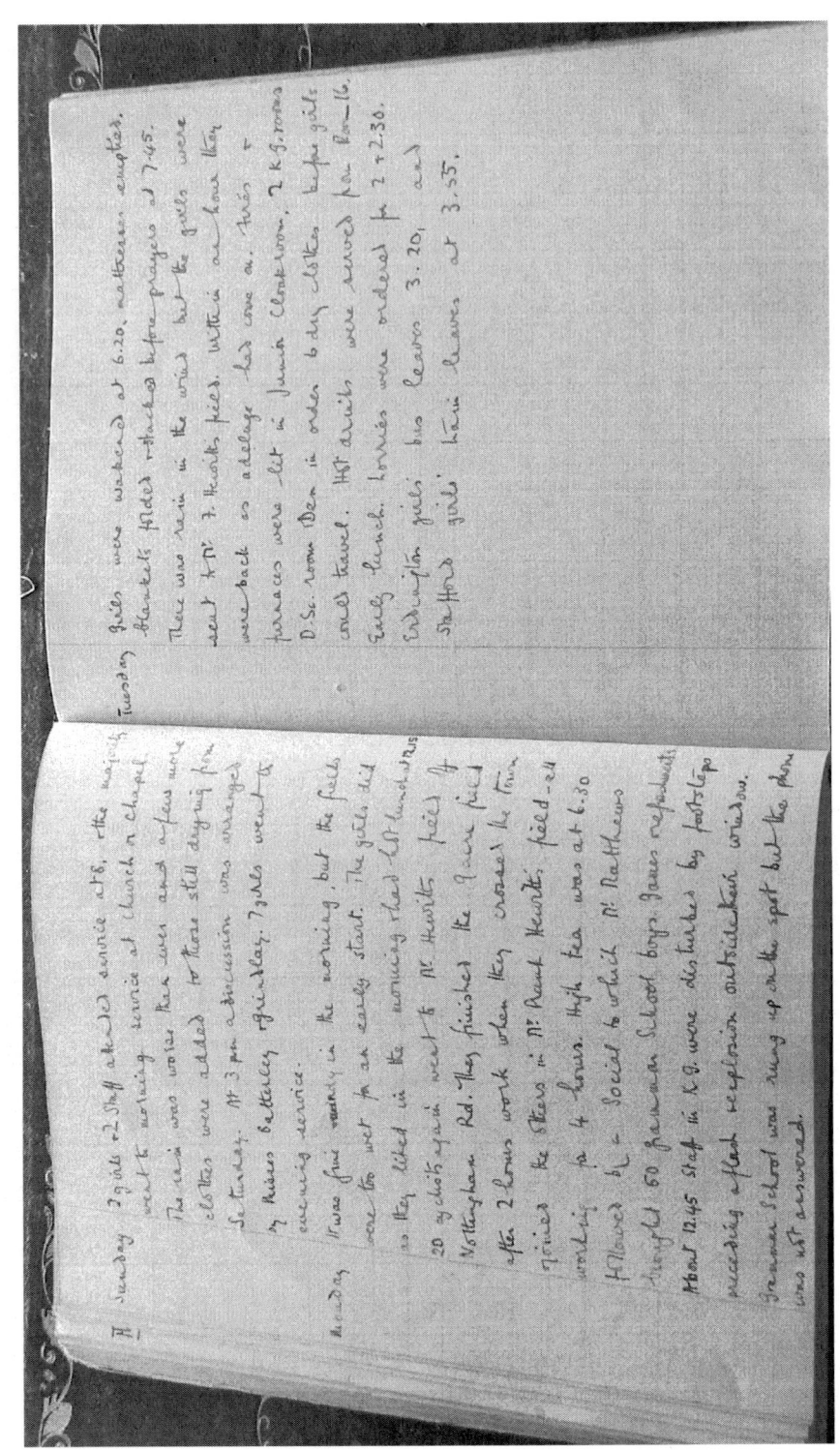

Sunday 19th August 1944

2 girls and 2 staff attended service at 8 and the majority went to the morning service at Church or Chapel. The rain was worse than ever and a few more clothes were added to those still drying from Saturday. At 3pm a discussion was arranged by Misses Batterley and Grindlay. 7 girls went to evening service.

Monday 20th August

It was fine and windy in the morning but the fields were too wet for an early start. The girls did as they liked in the morning and had hot lunch at 12.15. 20 cyclists again went to Mr Hewitt's field off Nottingham Rd. They finished the 9 acre field after 2 hours work when they crossed the town and joined the others in Mr Frank Hewitt's field – all working for 4 hours. High tea was at 6.30 followed by a social to which Mr Matthews brought 60 grammar school boys. Games, refreshments. About 12.45 staff in K. G. were disturbed by footsteps preceding a flash and explosion outside their window. Grammar school was rung up on the spot but the phone was not answered.

Tuesday 21st August

Girls were wakened at 6.20, mattresses emptied, blankets folded and stacked before prayers at 7.45. There was rain in the wind but the girls were sent to Mr Hewitt's field. Within an hour they were back as a deluge had come on. Fires and furnaces were lit in Junior cloakroom, 2 K.G. rooms D. Sc. room Den (sic) in order to dry clothes before girls could travel. Hot drinks were served from Room 16. Early Lunch. Lorries were ordered for 2 and 2.30. Erdington girls' bus leaves at 3.20 and Stafford girls' train leaves at 3.55.

Ashby de la Zouch Girls' Wartime Harvest Camps 1942-1944

Appendix 1.1 Roll Call 1942

Name	Sun.	Mon.	Tues.	Wed.	Thurs.	Fri.	Sat.
B Worrington	✓	✓	✓	✓	✓	✓	✓
A Pauler	✓	✓	✓	✓	✓	✓	✓
J Preston	✓	✓	✓	✓	✓	✓	✓
S Chambers	✓	✓	✓	✓	✓	✓	✓
P Best	✓	✓	✓	✓	✓	✓	✓
P Corden	✓	✓	✓	✓	✓	✓	✓
M Corden	✓	✓	✓	✓	✓	✓	✓
M Thorpe	✓	✓	✓	✓	✓	✓	✓
D Coxon	✓	✓	✓	✓	✓	✓	✓
G Kirby	✓	✓	✓	✓	✓	✓	✓
R Pulins	✓	✓	✓	✓	✓	✓	✓
D Vickers	✓	✓	✓	✓	✓	✓	✓
J Padbury	✓	✓	✓	✓	✓	✓	✓
S Smedley	✓	✓	✓	✓	✓	✓	✓
D Alestrock	✓	✓	✓	✓	✓	✓	✓
A Sabine	✓	✓	✓	✓	✓	✓	✓
E Hatton	✓	✓	✓	✓	✓	✓	✓
J Webb	✓	✓	✓	✓	✓	✓	✓
N Clay	✓	✓	✓	✓	✓	✓	✓
B Conway	✓	✓	✓	✓	✓	✓	✓
	20	20	20	20	20	20	20

Roll call, week 1, Sunday 16th August to Saturday 22nd August 1942

Roll call, week 2 Saturday 22nd August to Saturday 29th August 1942

Ashby de la Zouch Girls' Wartime Harvest Camps 1942-1944

Roll call week 3, Sunday 30th August to Saturday 5th September 1942

Roll call week 4, Monday 7th September to Saturday 12th September

Appendix 1.2 Hours and Earnings 1942

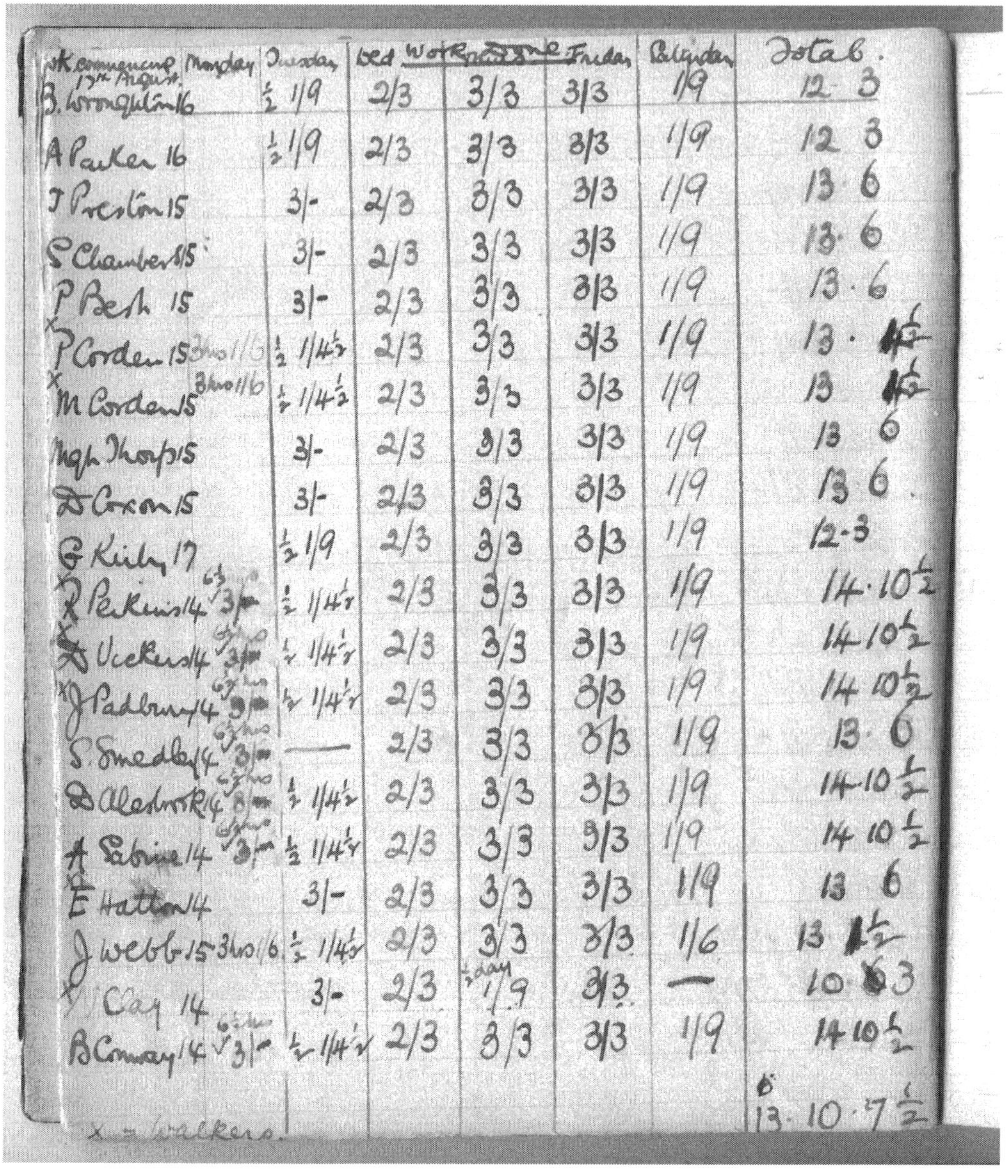

Wk commencing 17th August	Monday	Tuesday	Wed	Thursday	Friday	Saturday	Total
B. Wrongfulin 16		½ 1/9	2/3	3/3	3/3	1/9	12 3
A Parker 16		½ 1/9	2/3	3/3	3/3	1/9	12 3
J Preston 15		3/-	2/3	3/3	3/3	1/9	13 6
S Chambers 15		3/-	2/3	3/3	3/3	1/9	13 6
P Best 15		3/-	2/3	3/3	3/3	1/9	13·6
x P Corden 15	3hrs 1/6	½ 1/4½	2/3	3/3	3/3	1/9	13·4½
x M Corden 15	3hrs 1/6	½ 1/4½	2/3	3/3	3/3	1/9	13 4½
Mgt Thorp 15		3/-	2/3	3/3	3/3	1/9	13 6
D Coxon 15		3/-	2/3	3/3	3/3	1/9	13 6
G Kirby 17		½ 1/9	2/3	3/3	3/3	1/9	12·3
x R Perkins 14	6½ 3/-	½ 1/4½	2/3	3/3	3/3	1/9	14·10½
x D Vickers 14	6½hrs 3/-	½ 1/4½	2/3	3/3	3/3	1/9	14 10½
x J Padbury 14	6½hrs 3/-	½ 1/4½	2/3	3/3	3/3	1/9	14 10½
S Smedley 14	6½hrs 3/-	—	2/3	3/3	3/3	1/9	13 6
D Aldebrook 14	6½hrs 3/-	½ 1/4½	2/3	3/3	3/3	1/9	14-10½
A Sabine 14	6½hrs 3/-	½ 1/4½	2/3	3/3	3/3	1/9	14 10½
E Hatton 14		3/-	2/3	3/3	3/3	1/9	13 6
J Webb 15	3hrs 1/6	½ 1/4½	2/3	3/3	3/3	1/6	13 1½
V Clay 14		3/-	2/3	½ day 1/9	3/3	—	10 3
B Conway 14	6½hrs 3/-	½ 1/4½	2/3	3/3	3/3	1/9	14 10½
							£13·10·7½

x = walkers.

Earnings week 1, Monday 17th August to Saturday 22nd August 1942

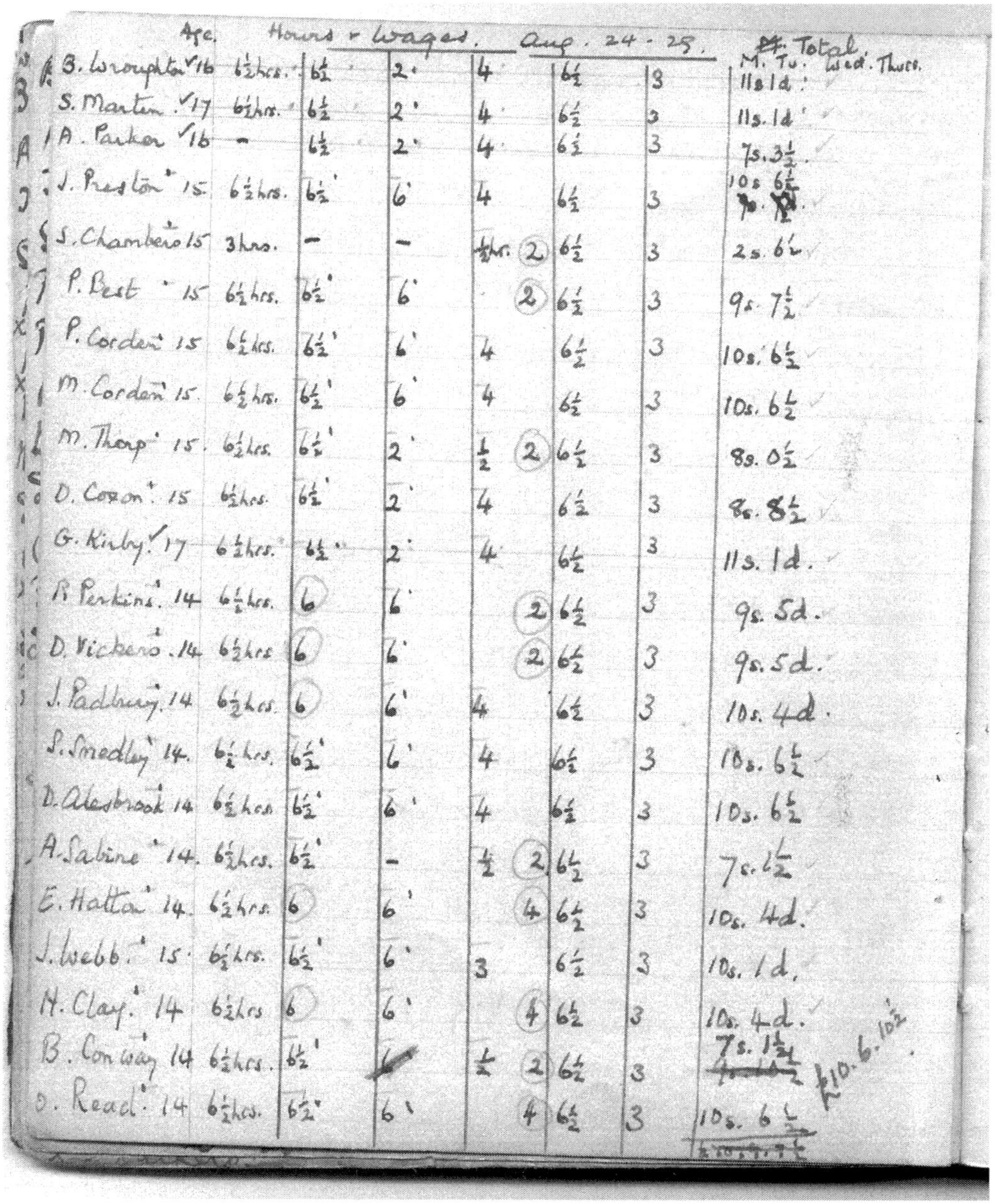

Name	Age		Hours + Wages. Aug. 24 - 29.					Total
			M.	Tu.	Wed.	Thurs.		
B. Wroughton	16	6½hrs.	6½	2	4	6½	3	11s 1d
S. Martin	17	6½hrs.	6½	2	4	6½	3	11s. 1d
A. Parker	16	–	6½	2	4	6½	3	7s. 3½
J. Preston	15	6½hrs.	6½	6	4	6½	3	10s 6½
S. Chambers	15	3hrs.	–	–	½hr. (2)	6½	3	2s. 6½
P. Best	15	6½hrs.	6½	6	(2)	6½	3	9s. 7½
P. Corden	15	6½hrs.	6½	6	4	6½	3	10s. 6½
M. Corden	15	6½hrs.	6½	6	4	6½	3	10s. 6½
M. Thorp	15	6½hrs.	6½	2	½ (2)	6½	3	8s. 0½
D. Coxon	15	6½hrs.	6½	2	4	6½	3	8s. 8½
G. Kirby	17	6½hrs.	6½	2	4	6½	3	11s. 1d.
R. Perkins	14	6½hrs.	(6)	6	(2)	6½	3	9s. 5d.
D. Vickers	14	6½hrs.	(6)	6	(2)	6½	3	9s. 5d.
J. Padbury	14	6½hrs.	(6)	6	4	6½	3	10s. 4d.
S. Smedley	14	6½hrs.	6½	6	4	6½	3	10s. 6½
D. Alesbrook	14	6½hrs.	6½	6	4	6½	3	10s. 6½
A. Sabine	14	6½hrs.	6½	–	½ (2)	6½	3	7s. 6½
E. Hatton	14	6½hrs.	(6)	6	(4)	6½	3	10s. 4d.
J. Webb	15	6½hrs.	6½	6	3	6½	3	10s. 1d.
H. Clay	14	6½hrs.	(6)	6	(4)	6½	3	10s. 4d.
B. Conway	14	6½hrs.	6½	~~6~~	½ (2)	6½	3	7s. 1½
O. Read	14	6½hrs.	6½	6	(4)	6½	3	10s. 6½
								£10. 6. 10½

Hours and earnings week 2,
Monday 24th August to Saturday 29th August 1942

Ashby de la Zouch Girls' Wartime Harvest Camps 1942-1944

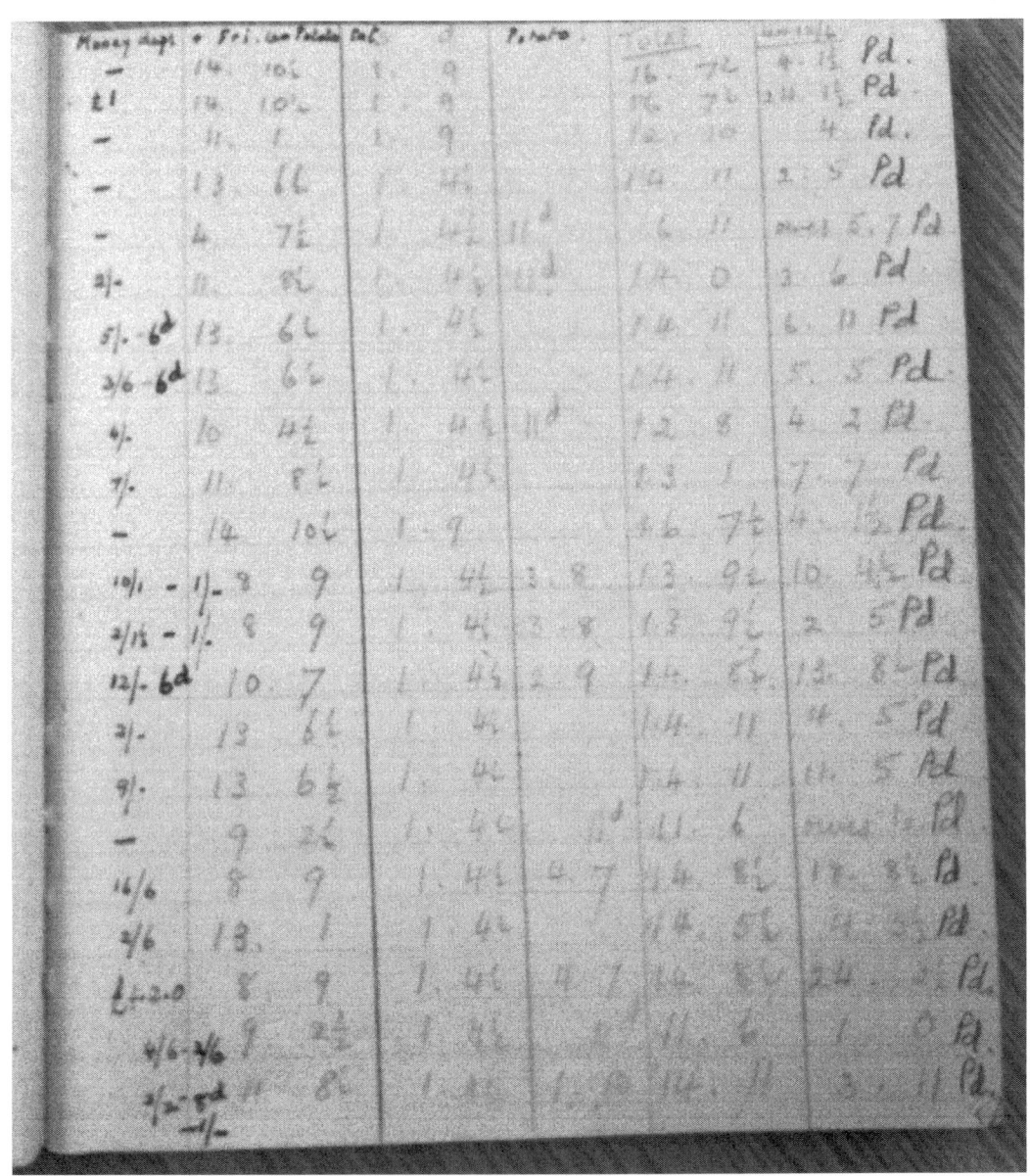

Hours and earnings week 2,
Monday 24th August to Saturday 29th August 1942
(continued from previous page)

*Money received from employers, week 2,
Monday 24th August to Saturday 29th August 1942*

Hours and earnings week 3
Monday August 31st to Saturday 5th September

Hours and earnings week 4,
Monday 7th September to Saturday 12th September

Appendix 1.3 Camp cash account 1942

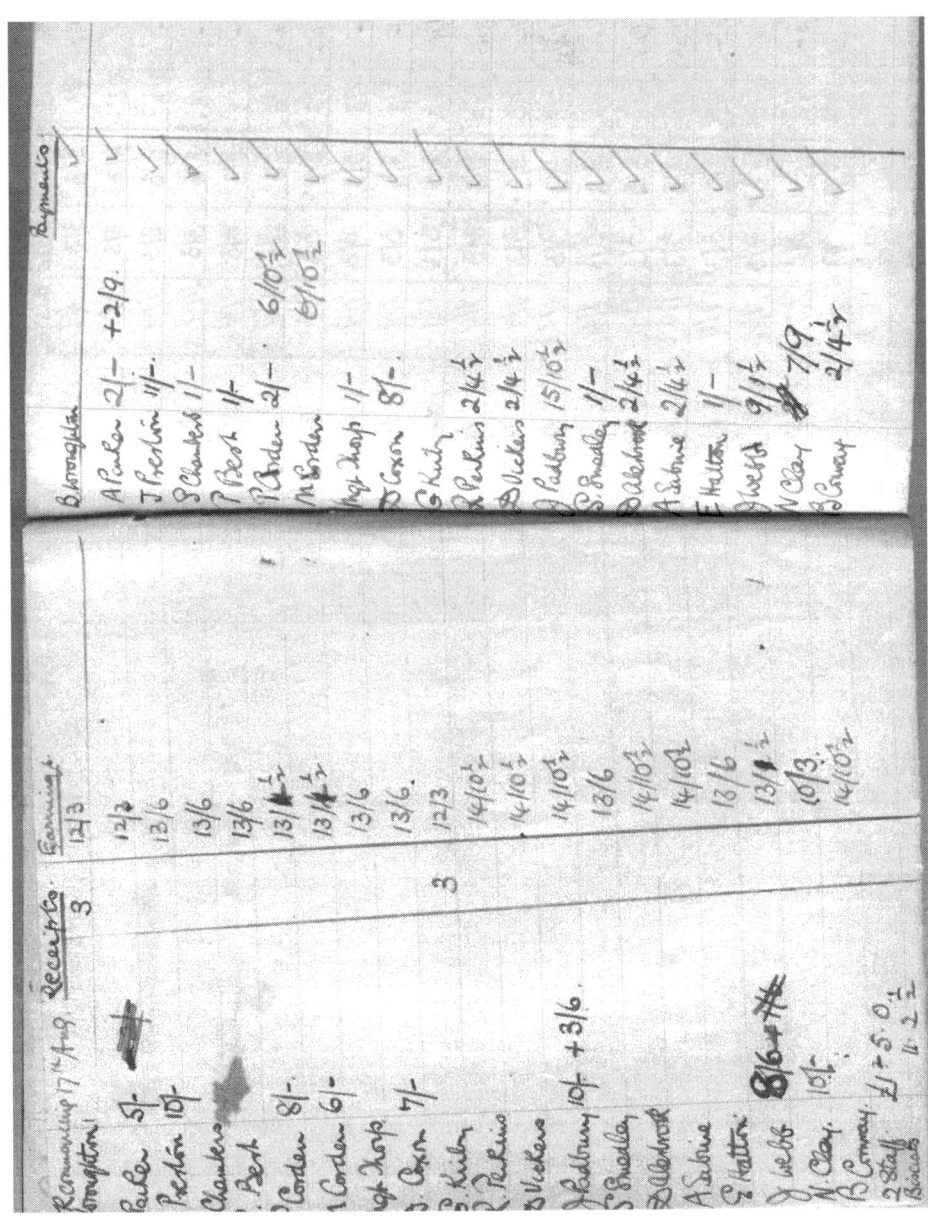

Receipts, earnings and payments to girls, week beginning 17th August 1942

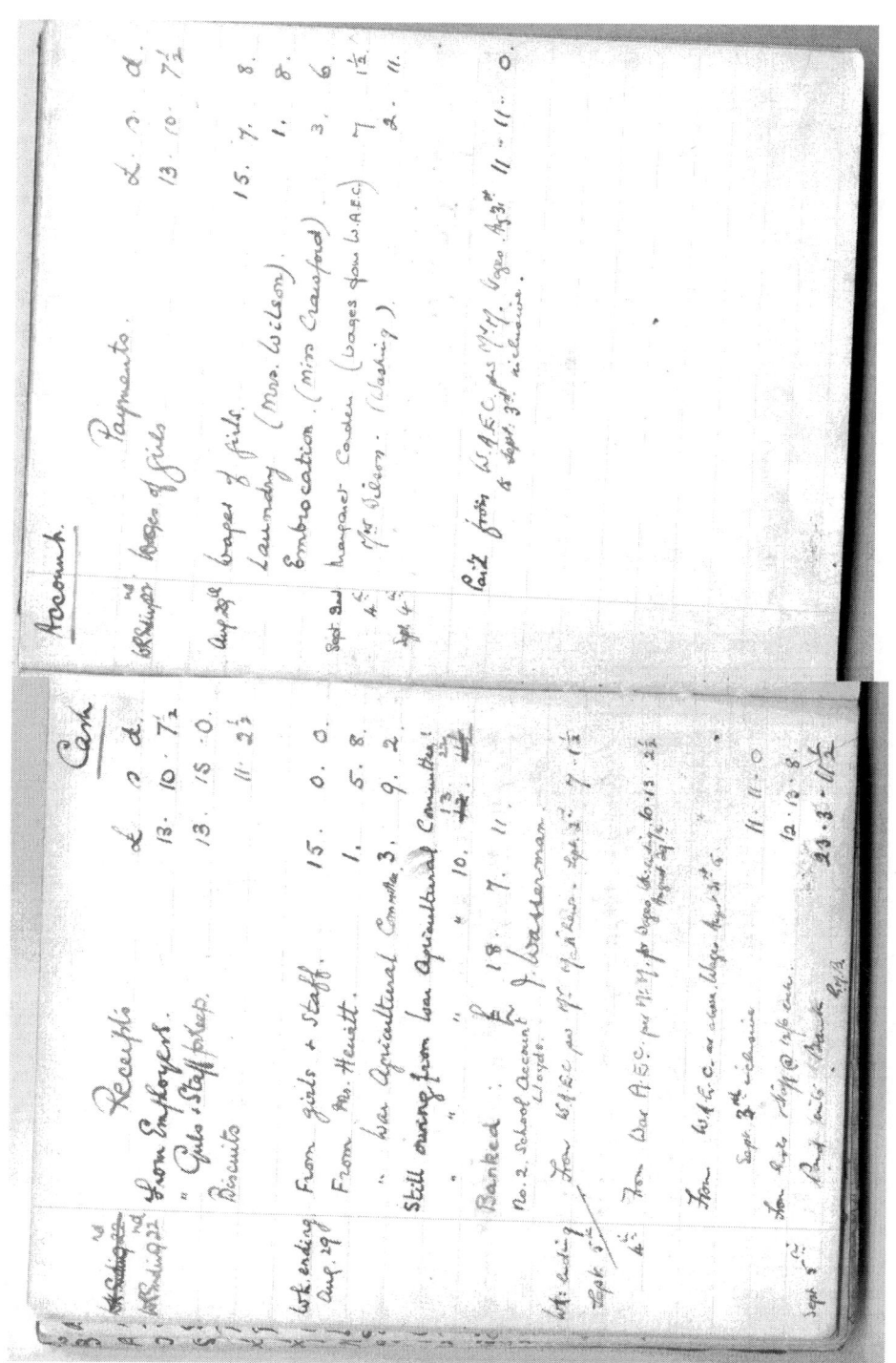

Cash account 1942 showing income and expenditure

Ashby de la Zouch Girls' Wartime Harvest Camps 1942-1944

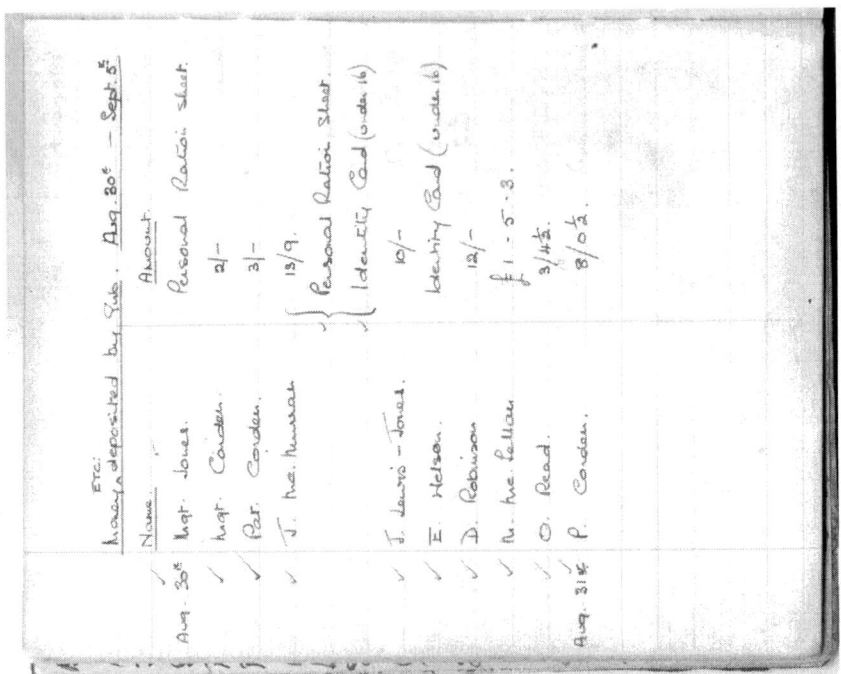

Monies and ration books deposited by girls Aug 30th – Sept 5th 1942

Cash Account – week ending Sat, Sept. 12th

Receipts.

		£	s	d
Sept. 11th	From W.A.E.C.	14	8	0½
Sept. 12th	From girls & staff for board at 12/6 each.	10	0	0
" 12th	From 14 girls, 2/5 each owing for last week's board.	1	13	10
" 12th	From W.A.E.C.	3	9	8
" 12th	Paid into Lloyds Bank, No. 2, School Account	11	15	2½

Left in chocolate box after deducting 4/8 for Mrs Wilson & 6d for telephone calls. 2/1½.

Payments.

	£	s	d
Sept. 12th a.m. Wages of girls	13	1	9
Sept. 12th p.m. Wages of girls	3	7	1½
Sept. 12th Mrs Wilson 3rd wk (for washing) 4th wk		1 3	4 4
Telephone calls.			6
Wages of 5 girls, at present unclaimed, to be paid out at beginning of term.	1	5	10

Receipts and expenditure Sept 11th – 12th 1942

Appendix 1.4 Orderlies and Field Work 1942

Orderlies and field work record Aug 31st – Sept 4th 1942

1942

Orderlies for Monday, Sept. 7 M. Cawston, J. Padbury, J. Mallaman, M. Maclellan
" " Tuesday, " 8 J. Lewis Jones, E. Nelson, P. Corden
" " Wednesday " 9 J. McMurran, M. Cawston, M. Ensor
" " Thursday " 10 J. Martin, E. Nelson, J. Webb
" " Friday " 11 J. Padbury, M. Cawston, J. Fairhead
" " Saturday " 12 P. Corden, E. Wing, E. Nelson

Field Supervision.
Monday, a.m. Miss Good, p.m. Miss Bayford.
Tuesday, a.m. " " p.m. " "
Wednesday, a.m. " " p.m. " "
Thursday, a.m. " " p.m. " "
Friday, a.m. " Bayford, p.m. " Good.
Saturday a.m. " Good. p.m. —

Field Work.
Mon. — Thurs. inclusive, flax-pulling at Otterwell's farm, Nottingham Rd. Pulling finished at 12.15 p.m., Friday. Shocking in afternoon, — about ⅓ of field, perhaps a little more.
Sat. — flax-pulling for Mr. Knight, Packington, 9.30 a.m. — 12.30 p.m.

Orderlies and field work record Sept 7th – Sept 12th 1942

Ashby de la Zouch Girls' Wartime Harvest Camps 1942-1944

Appendix 2.1 Roll call 1943

Roll call August 7th – 14th 1943

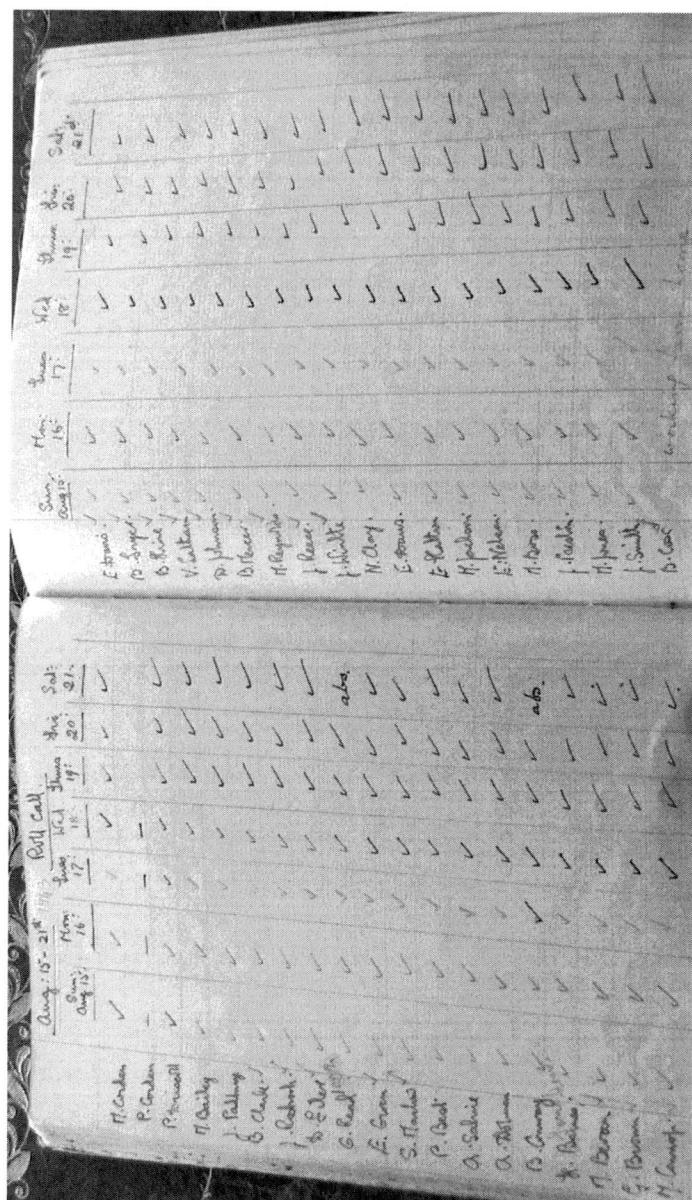
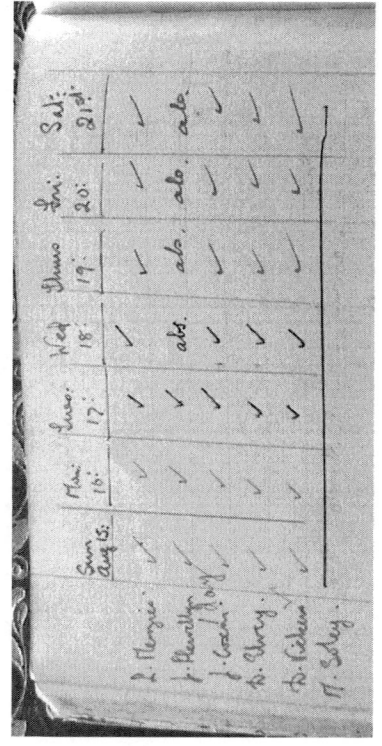

Roll call August 15th – 21st 1943

Ashby de la Zouch Girls' Wartime Harvest Camps 1942-1944

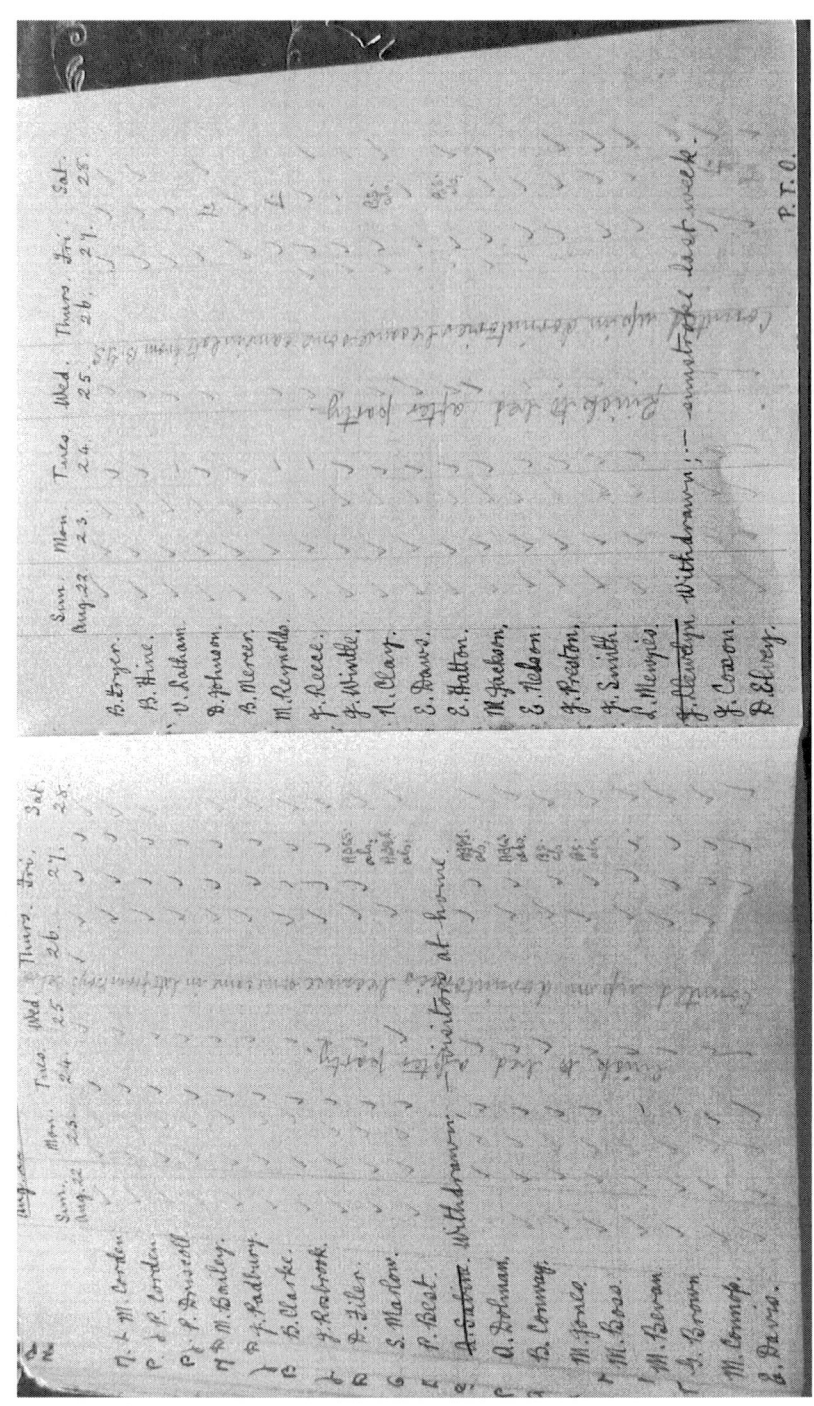

Roll call August 22nd – 28th 1943

Roll call August 22nd – 28th 1943 continued

Ashby de la Zouch Girls' Wartime Harvest Camps 1942-1944

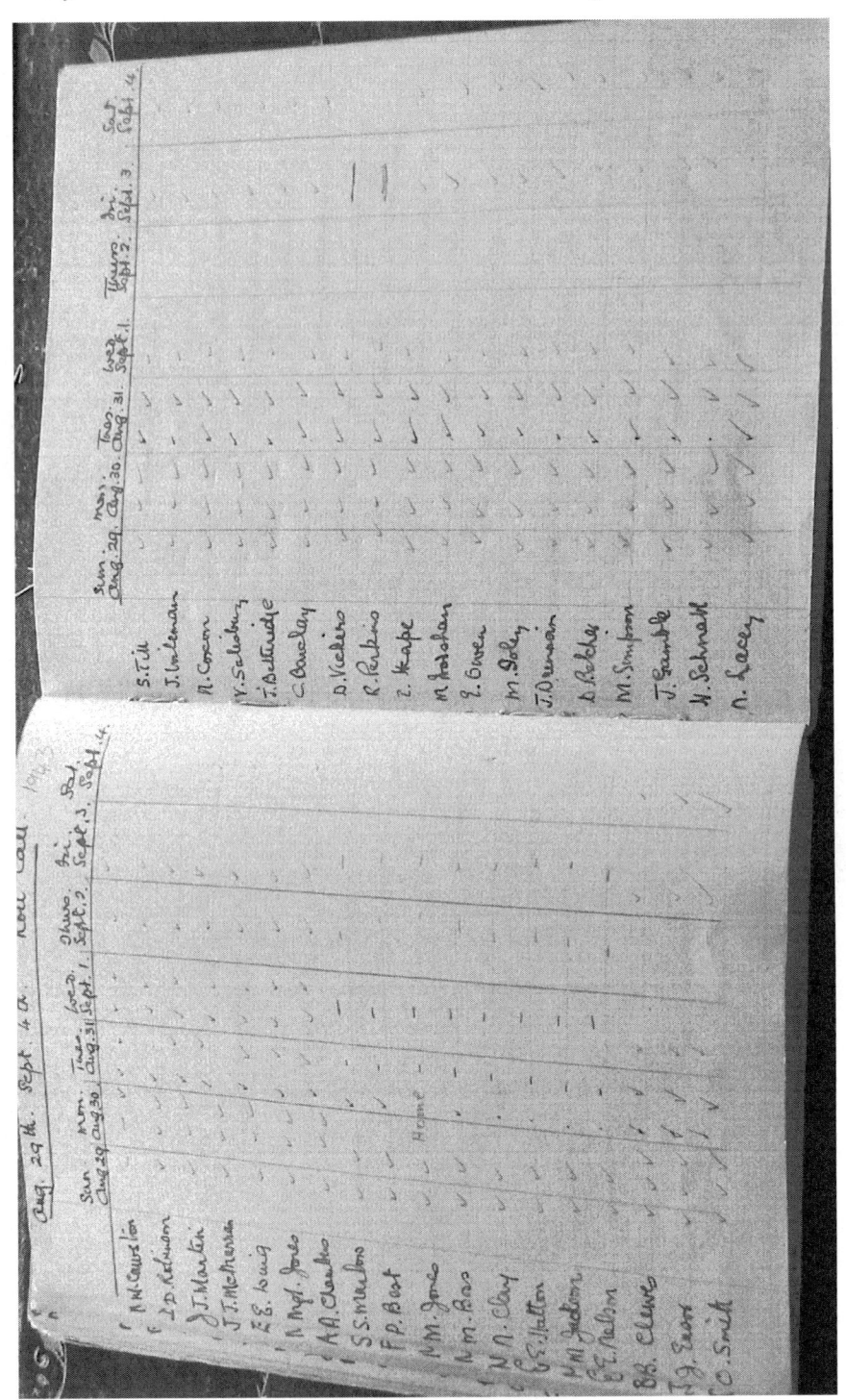

Roll call 29th Aug – 4th Sept 1943

Appendix 2.2 Hours and Earnings 1943

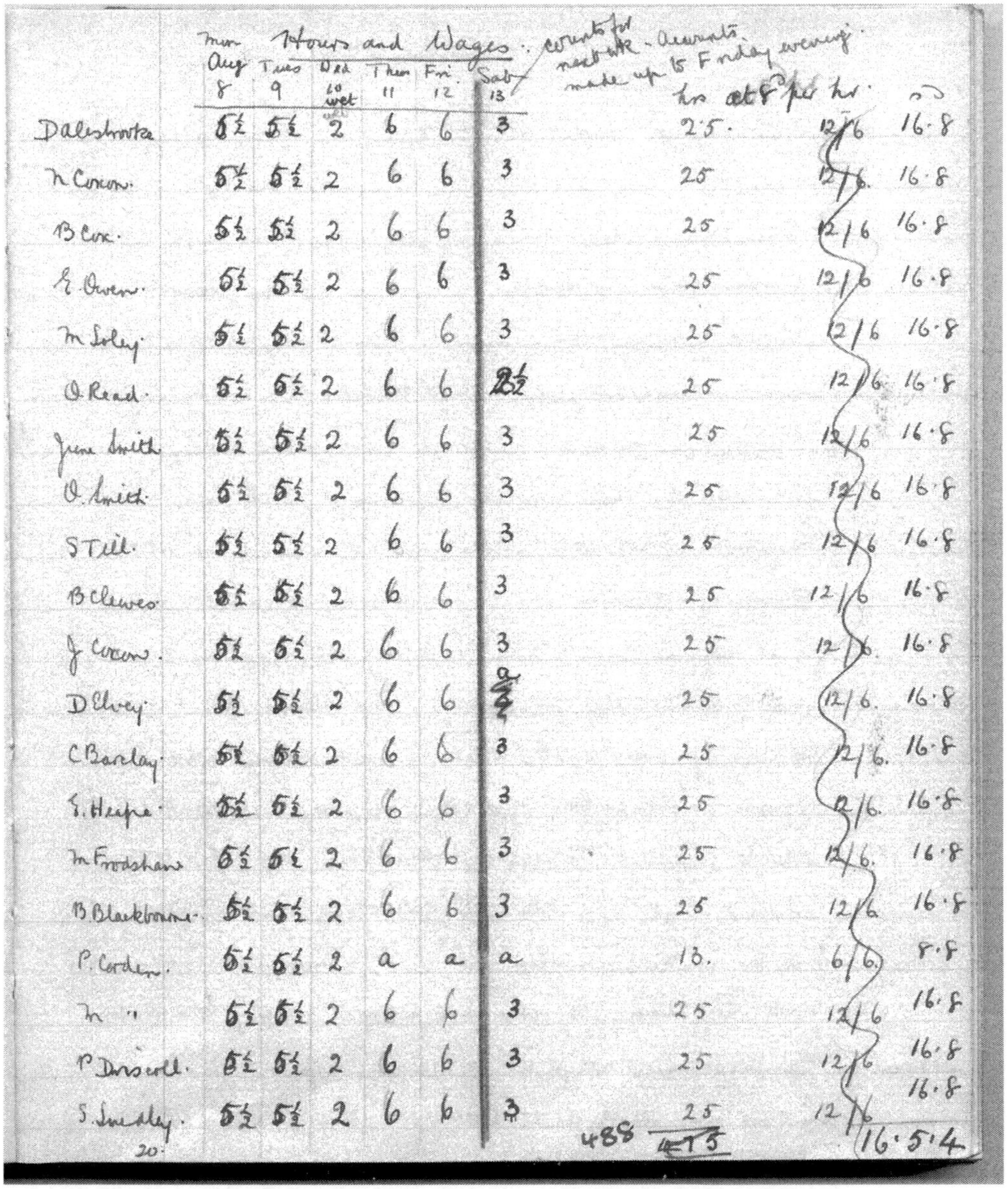

Name	Mon Aug 8	Tues 9	Wed 10 wet	Thurs 11	Fri 12	Sat 13		hrs at 8 per hr	
D Aleshinska	5½	5½	2	6	6	3	25	12/6	16.8
N Coxon	5½	5½	2	6	6	3	25	12/6	16.8
B Cox	5½	5½	2	6	6	3	25	12/6	16.8
E Owen	5½	5½	2	6	6	3	25	12/6	16.8
M Soley	5½	5½	2	6	6	3	25	12/6	16.8
O Read	5½	5½	2	6	6	2½	25	12/6	16.8
June Smith	5½	5½	2	6	6	3	25	12/6	16.8
O Smith	5½	5½	2	6	6	3	25	12/6	16.8
S Till	5½	5½	2	6	6	3	25	12/6	16.8
B Clewes	5½	5½	2	6	6	3	25	12/6	16.8
J Coxon	5½	5½	2	6	6	3	25	12/6	16.8
D Elvey	5½	5½	2	6	6	a	25	12/6	16.8
C Barley	5½	5½	2	6	6	3	25	12/6	16.8
S Heape	5½	5½	2	6	6	3	25	12/6	16.8
M Frodsham	5½	5½	2	6	6	3	25	12/6	16.8
B Blackbourne	5½	5½	2	6	6	3	25	12/6	16.8
P Corden	5½	5½	2	a	a	a	13	6/6	8.8
M "	5½	5½	2	6	6	3	25	12/6	16.8
P Driscoll	5½	5½	2	6	6	3	25	12/6	16.8
S Smedley	5½	5½	2	6	6	3	25	12/6	16.8
20							488		16.5.4

Hours worked and earnings August 8th – 12th 1943

Ashby de la Zouch Girls' Wartime Harvest Camps 1942-1944

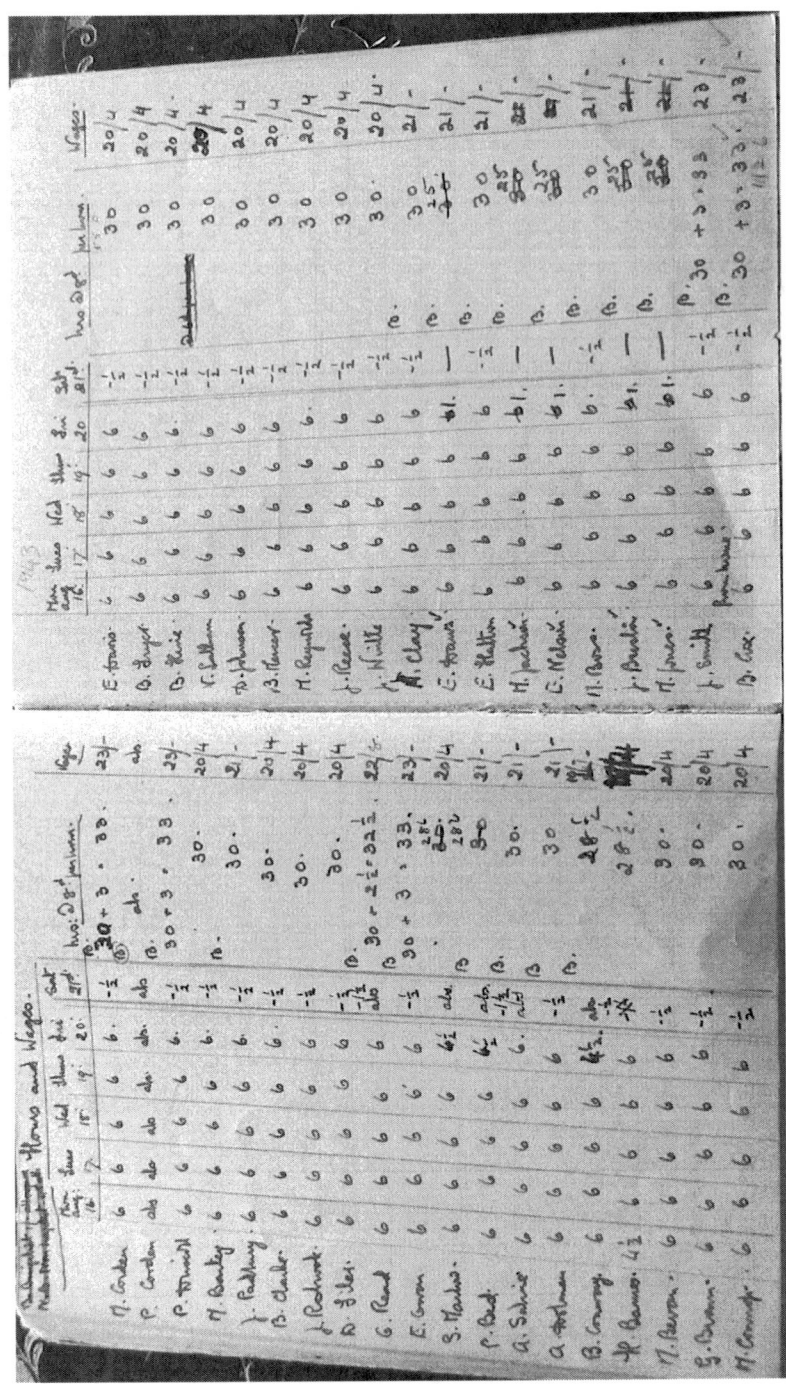

Hours worked and earnings August 16th – 21st 1943

Continuation of hours worked and earnings August 16th – 21st 1943

Ashby de la Zouch Girls' Wartime Harvest Camps 1942-1944

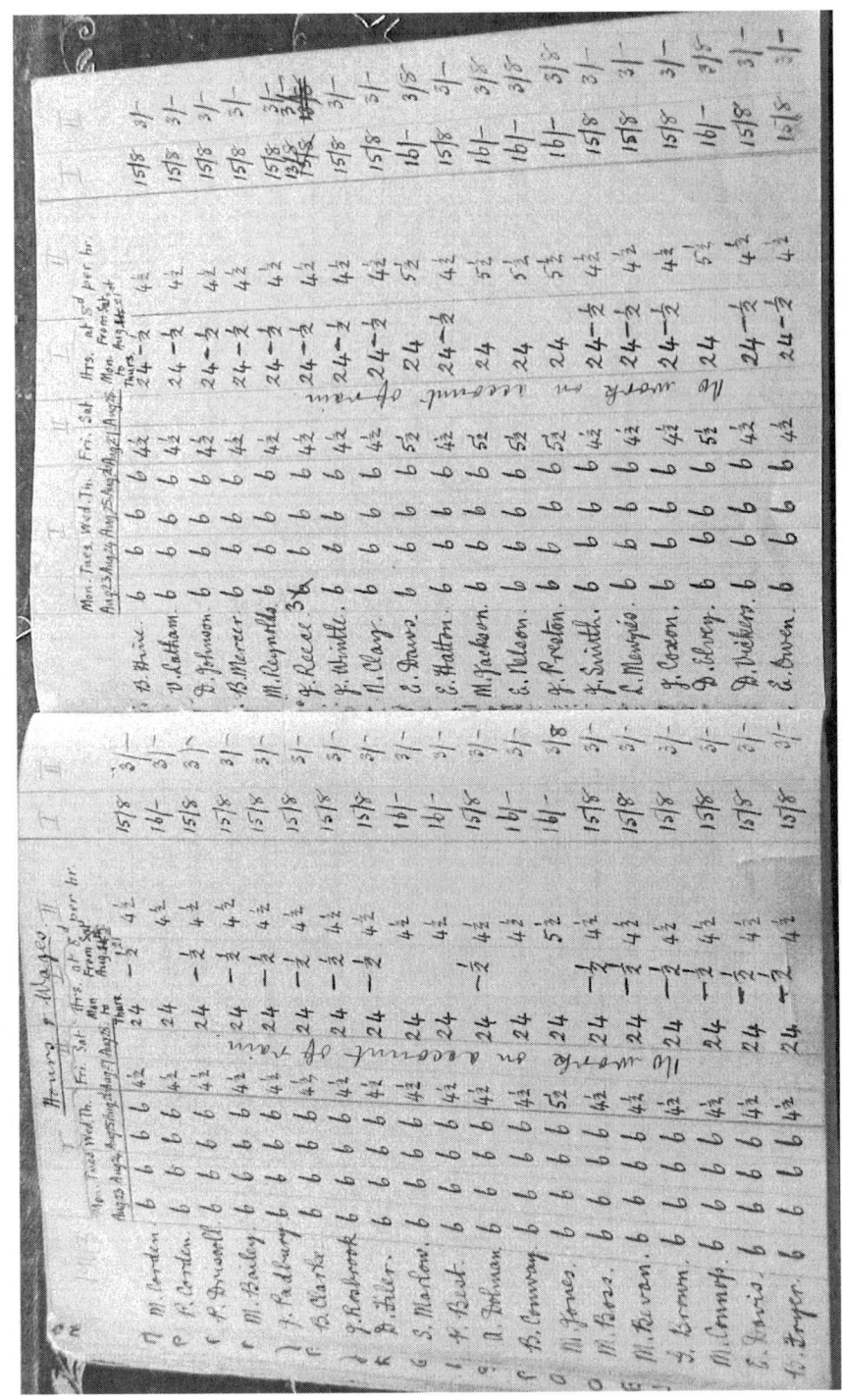

Hours worked and earnings August 23rd – 28th 1943

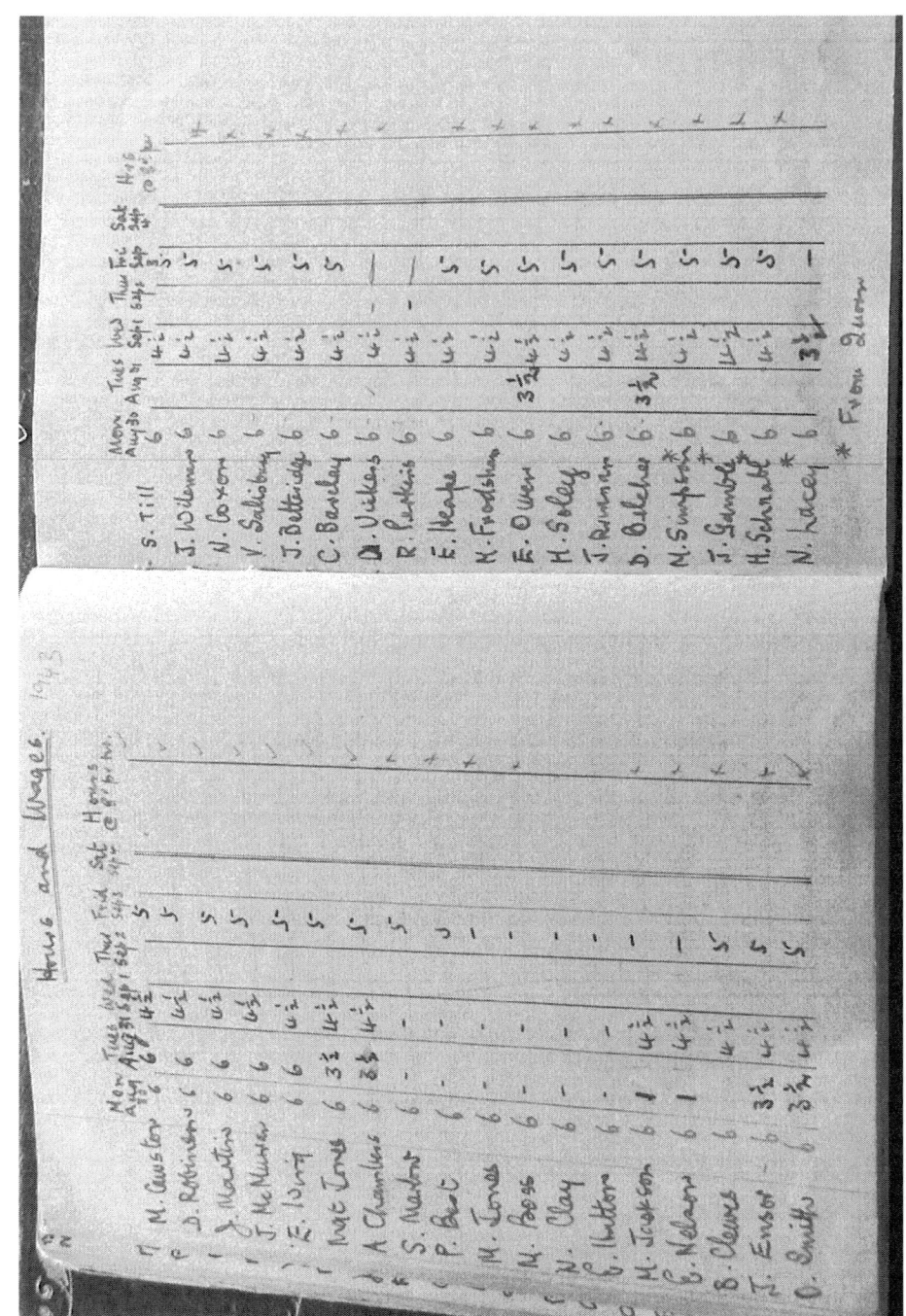

Hours worked and earnings August 30th – September 4th 1943

Ashby de la Zouch Girls' Wartime Harvest Camps 1942-1944

	Mon Aug 30	Tues Aug 31	Wed Sept 1	Thur Sep 2	Fri Sep 3	Sat Sep 4
M S. Smedley	6		4½		5	
D.D. Alesbrook	6		4½		5	
J. J. Brown	6		4½		5	
J. E. Bramwell	6		4½		5	
E O. Read	6		4½		5	

Hours worked and earnings August 30th – September 4th 1943
Continued from the previous page

Appendix 2.3 Camp Cash Account 1943

Money deposited 1943

Ashby de la Zouch Girls' Wartime Harvest Camps 1942-1944

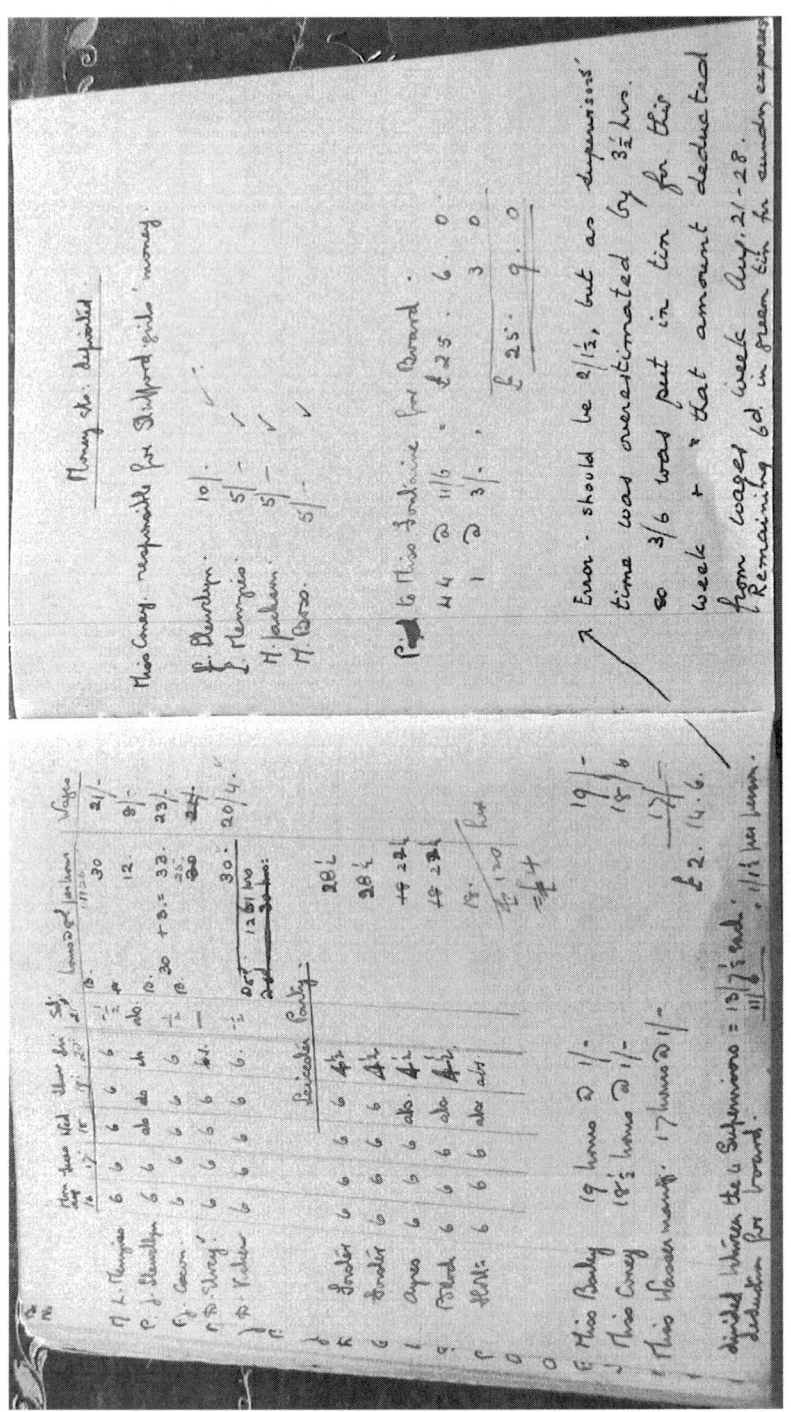

Money deposited August 16th – 21st 1943

Wendy Freer

Money, etc., deposited.	Drawn out.
S. Martin £2. 0. 0	
J. Baker. £1. 0. 0	
J. Padbury. 12. 0	
P. Corden. 16. 0	
M. Corden £1. 5. 0	
E. Halton. 6. 0	
N. Clay. 6. 0	
E. Heape. 4. 6 (Leaving camp Fri. eve). +18/-(wages)+2/-	1/- & 4/- £1.4.6 − 11/6 = 13/-
M. Jones. 6. 0	
M. Frodsham. 4. 0 +1/-	5/-
C. Menzies. 10. 0	
B. Blackburn. 6. 5 (Leaving camp Fri. eve). +18/- wages +2/-	£1.6.5 − 11/6 = 14/11
M. Connop. 10. 0	6d 1/- 6d
M. Bevan. 8. 6 (wages in Bank bag) 17. 6 (in purse).	4/- 1/- 1/-
J. Reece. 3. 0	1/- 1/- 1/-

Money deposited 22ⁿᵈ August – 29ᵗʰ august

Ashby de la Zouch Girls' Wartime Harvest Camps 1942-1944

> Money etc. deposited.
>
> N. Clay — 7/9 — returned
> L. Hatton — 7/3 — returned
> E. Nelson — 10/-
> O. Smith — 5/6½ — 5/0½
> J. Wileman — 9/3
> U. Coxon — 5/-
> J. Drennan — £1.0.8¾
> D. Belcher — 2/3½
> M. Simpson — 10/-
> J. Gamble — 6/5
> N. Schnabl — 14/3 — 10/3
> N. Lacey — 18/1½
> M. Soley — 9/9
> J. Ensor — 5/1½

Money deposited 1943

Appendix 2.4 Orderlies 1943

Orderlies							
Hall (2)	Monday	Tues	Wed	Thurs	Fri	Sat	
Jean Smith	Tidying	Sandwiches	Supper	Breakfast	Tidying	Sandwich	
Doreen Ivey	Sandwich	Supper	Breakfast	Tidying	Sandwich	Supper	
Nancy Cocon	Supper	Breakfast	Tidying	Sandwiches	Supper	Breakfast	
June Cocon	Breakfast	Tidying	Sandwiches	Supper	Breakfast	Tidying	

Hall (1)	Monday	Tues	Wed	Thurs	Fri	Sat
Olive Smith	Room	Same as Monday	Supper	Breakfast	Same as Thurs	
Brenda Cleaves	Supper		Breakfast	Supper		
Sheila Till	Breakfast		Tidy	Supper		

K.G. — for week.
- Room Orderly — Olive Read.
- Sandwich — Edna Owen.
- Dinner — Mgt Frodsham.
- Breakfast — Elaine Heape.

Orderlies 1943

Ashby de la Zouch Girls' Wartime Harvest Camps 1942-1944

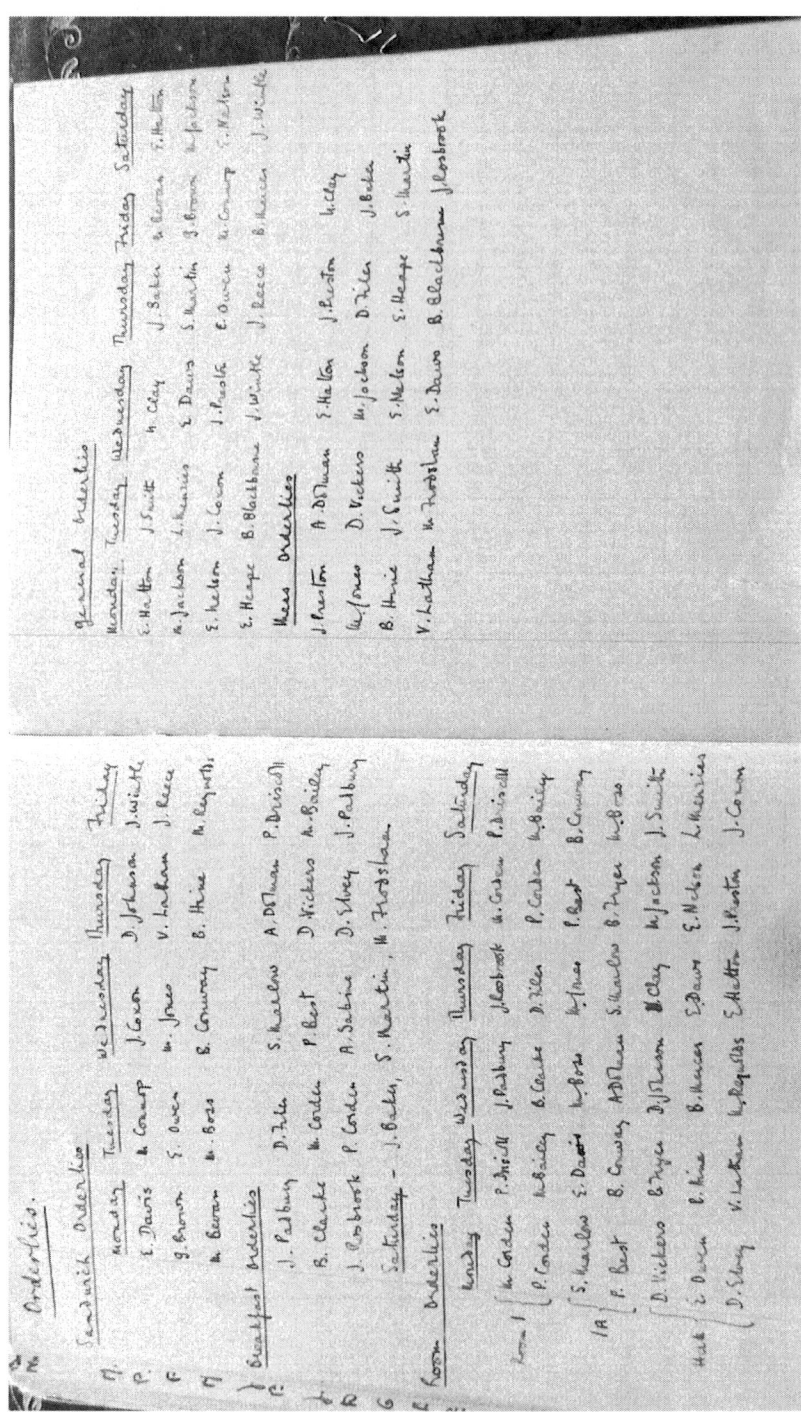

Orderlies 1943

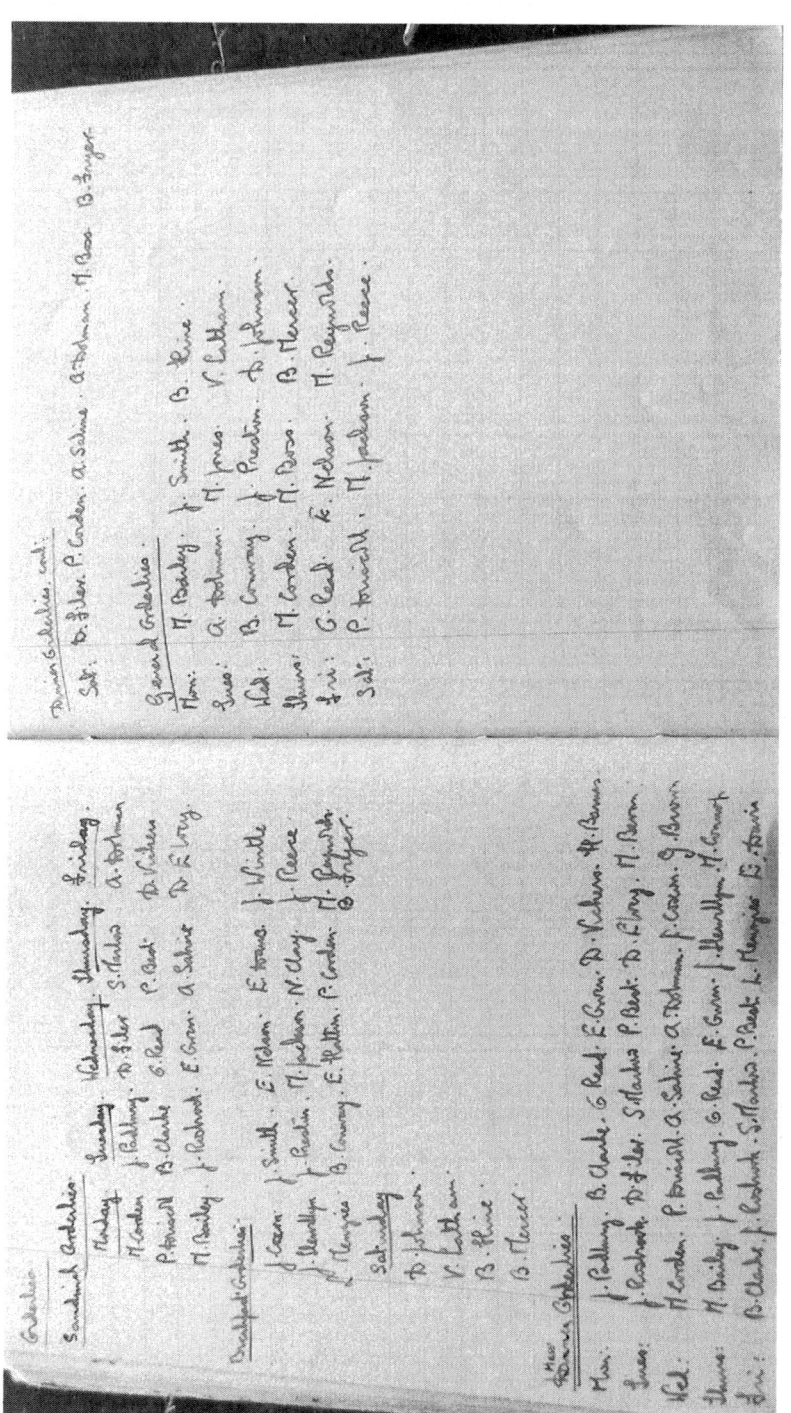

Orderlies 1943